VIRGINIA & TRUCKEE

A STORY OF VIRGINIA CITY AND COMSTOCK TIMES

BY

LUCIUS BEEBE

AND

CHARLES CLEGG

Decorations by
E. S. HAMMACK

Maps and Lettering by
FREDERIC SHAW

Published by

NEVADA STATE RAILROAD MUSEUM

2180 S. Carson Street / Carson City, Nevada 89710 / Telephone (702) 687-6953

PREFACE TO THE FIFTH EDITION

When the original copy of this modest volume was prepared for its first printing nearly a decade and a half ago, the Virginia & Truckee Railroad was still a going concern. Its occasions were of modest consequence to Nevadans who had not then and, indeed, have not even now achieved the stage of maturity that elsewhere is indicated by an appreciation of the remarkable and important past, but the V&T in the final years of its operation was already an object of compelling interest to antiquarians and railroad amateurs. While time was running out for the carrier, it was already Nevada's most celebrated tangible institution and, while the greedy heirs of the Mills Estate clamored for the value in junk of the railroad that had made them, both directly and by indirection, rich, it was becoming the most famous short line in the world.

When the end came, as it must for all things, to the Virginia & Truckee, it came splendidly after eighty full years of usefulness and romance. Full of honors and leaving behind its final going remembered fragrances of glory, its physical properties entered the roundhouses of history, but its soul, and if any inanimate thing can be credited with a soul it is a ship or a railroad, went marching on. In its lifetime, the V&T enjoyed wealth, celebrity and admiration beyond the ordinary; in death it achieved a radiant immortality. Its memory has been kept green by a bibliography that might be the envy of many a mainline. Its operations flourish amidst the gunsmoke of Culver City Westerns in cinema and on television. Its name is perpetuated throughout Nevada by V&T museums, motels, restaurants and the artifacts of tourist trade, paperweights, lithographs, book ends made from its burnished English rails and books like this. There is not, be it said to their glory, a saloon in Nevada that doesn't display in some form the pictured likeness of the once splendid Virginia & Truckee Railroad.

Thus, in a sense, the new printing of this slim volume of tribute is but the act of putting up the markers indicating another extra run on the smokebox of belles-lettres. In death the V&T is still in operation, its train movements characterized by enduring archaism, its whistle clearly audible from beyond the marge of Acheron. When it ceased to be a public carrier it became an article of faith. The Virginia & Truckee was and still enduringly is quite a railroad.

Virginia City
1963

LUCIUS BEEBE
CHARLES M. CLEGG

IN THE RICH and enduring lexicon of the old American West, the roll-call of its resources and tally of its wonderments, no names are more fragrant with romance and high destinies than the now ghostly place names and institutional names of Nevada. Topping the list will be that of Virginia City, scene of the Comstock Lode, the most prodigious bonanza in the history of the world and one by comparison to which the mines of King Solomon and the wealth of the Incas, even the legendary fame of El Dorado and Golconda, pale to insignificance.

And there are others in this scroll of mighty doings: Gould and Curry, Best and Belcher, Yellow Jacket, Con. Virginia, Ophir, Crown Point, mines of incredible richness and glittering memories. And there are still others: Carson City, Washoe, Central Pacific, Territorial Enterprise, Mormon Station, Gold Hill, Six Mile Canyon, the Geiger Grade, the Truckee Meadows, the pools of Sandy Bowers. All are significant of commotional doings in the heroic past.

And there is Virginia and Truckee, golden railroad to yesterday, the railroad which made possible the Big Bonanza, the railroad whose bright fame for decades was outshone only by the names of the mines themselves whose wealth it carried down to the mills on the Carson River. The mills, whose stacks and towering battlements once made a metropolis along the river shore as dense as the mills of Pittsburgh today, are now vanished in the desert more completely than the traces of Carthage or the nine cities of Troy.

Yet only yesterday their smoke ascended in towering clouds above the summit of Mount Davidson, the implications of their thundering stamps in an eccentric rigadoon of riches were audible to the ends of the earth. Pause, philosopher, by the margins of Carson and reflect on the dusty destinies of mankind. The rivers of Babylon where the Israelites sat them down and wept were no more eloquent of departed mightiness.

This is the story of a railroad so endowed with romance and wealthy destinies as to have become a legend in its own lifetime, an integral portion of the greatest of all pioneering sagas, the *matiere* of the old American West. It was once the richest railroad in the world measured in terms of return upon its investment and in the tangible assets it transported. Its traffic was in fabulous ores almost to the exclusion of all else. Its passengers and the arbiters of its operations were kings, more powerful in the symbolism of their Prince Albert frock coats than many anointed heads surmounted by historic crowns. Its terrain and domain were and, eighty years after its first flowering, still are among the grand and lonely regions of the habitable earth.

Sing, therefore, O Muse of Tractive Force and Valve Gear, of the Virginia and Truckee, a railroad of such superlatives that, like the Comstock it served and the San Francisco it enriched, its name will be forever currency in the language of the trans-Mississippi.

An English philosopher contemporary with the flowering years of Virginia City and the Comstock, Herbert Spencer, evolved the metaphysical theory that every act in life and history is the direct and unavoidable result of every act which has preceded it, and by this token the V & T was the direct and unavoidable result of the prospecting in 1859 on the eastern slopes of Mount Davidson in the then Territory of Western Utah of four boozy and disreputable scoundrels who found the world-shaking Comstock Lode. Two of them were Peter O'Reilly and Pat McLaughlin who uncovered the first specimens, and a third was a blackmailer and freebooter of impressive manner and sanctimonious pretentions named Henry Comstock who declared them to have done their prospecting on his property and cut himself in on a good thing. The fourth was a tosspot and tavern valiant named James Finney, popularly known as "Old Virginny" from his claims to birth in aristocratic circumstances in the Old Dominion. One night, early in the history of the Comstock, this prophetic ancient was taken in wine and, on the way home to his shack, tripped and fell, smashing a bottle of whisky he was carrying as a precaution against the night air and altitude. Reluctant to let the liquor disappear into the elemental earth without having some good of it, he turned the catastrophe into a christening party and then and there named the tent town Virginia City.

Tidings of precious metals in Nevada were nothing new to the Mother Lode. As early as 1850 a William H. Moore of Indiana, who had driven the first wagon ever to cross the plains from St. Joseph to California, reported a number of prospectors digging for gold in Carson Valley but that the biggest single piece of ore he had heard reported was worth no more than $15. But when it was reported on the strength of reliable assays that the samples of "blue stuff," long discarded by miners on the east side of Mount Davidson as worthless, ran to several thousand dollars a ton in silver the rush which, a decade before, had carried the tide of fortune seekers westward over the Sierra was reversed and the greatest wave of adventurers the world has ever known suddenly deserted the diggings of the Mother Lode and rolled eastward to the Washoe.

Caught up in this mighty landfaring were such millionaires to be as John Mackay, Senator George Hearst, Adolph Sutro, James Graham Fair, Senator John P. Jones, Sandy Bowers, Jim Flood, Jack O'Brien, and mighty, bearded Senator William M. Stewart, perhaps the most persistent of all Nevada seekers and finders who was to see the rushes to Virginia

City and to the Reese, to the White Pine, to Panamint, to Tonopah and Goldfield and, at long last, to the ultimate bonanza of them all, Bullfrog, above the incredible wastes of the Amargosa, well after the turn of the twentieth century.

They came by the roaring thousands, on mule back and afoot, a few in Concord coaches over the old grade by Hangtown and Strawberry and Carson City: the wicked and the willful, the soiled and solvent, the gyps and the gunmen, the splendid strumpets and blowzy madames, the gamblers, the newspaper reporters, kings and clowns. Wells Fargo came, the Bank of California came and, eventually, the railroad came, which is the concern of this story.

In the tumultuous decade that followed, Virginia and the Comstock, whose precincts by then included Gold Hill and Silver City as well as a fantastic array of mills and reducing plants along Six Mile Canyon, had several times been through the cycle of boom and bust. Virginia had exploded into a city of 20,000 wildly irresponsible inhabitants and the fame of its wicked ways, its continued uproar and production of stupefying wealth were celebrated throughout the civilized world. San Francisco in the decade following the discoveries of '49 was but a port of entry and financial center for the mining camps of the Mother Lode, and so it was with Virginia; but with her local banks Virginia was these things to the Comstock and, in addition, was the Comstock itself. Its banks and counting houses, agencies of the large San Francisco firms, were located on top of the very mine shafts that gave them birth and the twenty-four-hour-a-day civilization which flowered prodigiously on the slopes of Sun Mountain was like nothing which history had ever before recorded.

Virginia City sprawled wantonly and alluringly like Semiramis on the walls of Babylon. Throughout the early sixties its mine whistles screeched, its hoists clattered, its engines rumbled, dynamite boomed underground, gunfire exploded above ground, coaches clattered and ten thousand stamps in the stamping mills of Six Mile Canyon and along the Carson River thundered in a wild pavanne of prosperity. To the tune called by Virginia's mine superintendents stock booms mushroomed and collapsed on the exchanges and bourses of the world, a great civil war was fought to a conclusion generally felt to be satisfactory, San Francisco became the glittering jewel of the Pacific, and in far away Fifth Avenue alarming mansions were rising, turreted, machicolated, and crenelated, furnished in gilt and mirrors, plush and ormolu, with ballrooms, picture galleries and conservatories like visions in a mince-pie dream of the General Grant era. The mines of the Comstock paid for all of them.

But all was not well in the Comstock. The mine superintendents knew it, the market riggers in San Francisco's Montgomery Street knew it and when, in 1865, everyone knew it, Virginia suffered its first major stroke of mining apoplexy. The surface outcroppings were worked out; machinery for working the deeper stopes and winzes was prohibitively costly. Timber for shoring up the oppressive weight of Sun Peak in the galleries underground was getting scarce, and all sorts of unpleasant things like intrusions of boiling water and rock formations which flowed like liquid were being encountered at the lower levels. Miners were off by the hundred to the newly discovered strikes in the Reese River region and the White Pine Mountains of Eastern Nevada, and the word was getting about that the Comstock was mined out.

In this parlous pass confusion and dismay were on every hand.

Where to turn? What to do?

In the offices of the all-powerful Bank of California in San Francisco and the bank's agency of Virginia City's C Street as the seventh decade of the nineteenth century drew to an ominous close there were men who knew very precisely what to do to reanimate the Comstock, to make it profitable to work the most reluctant mines and, at one and the same time, achieve for themselves a concentration of wealth and power that were to become legendary. These men were William C. Ralston, cashier, and Darius Ogden Mills, president of the Bank of California, and their Virginia representative, William Sharon. Sharon, later United States Senator from Nevada and even now a kingmaker in broadcloth, was a scholarly, fastidious little man, an orator who quoted Shakespeare and Catullus at political rallies and a *bon viveur* who could identify the vineyard of its origin of the most recherché Moselle at a sniff of its cork. He was also a practitioner of financial legerdemain to whose ambition no term or boundary had ever yet been established.

Sharon, to whose private ear came every smidge of information and rumor concerning the Comstock, contemplated a marble bust of the Bard in his private office in Virginia City and knew with a great knowing that the Comstock wasn't worked out, wasn't in fact even scratched on the surface even though the main shafts of Gould and Curry and Crown Point and the Mexican were already down to the 700-foot level. These were mere surface bonanzas that had been uncovered by obvious and unsophisticated mining methods and men who were greedy for a quick killing with no eye to the great main chance. Why, due to their rapacious inefficiency in discarding low assay ores, there were even now millions in silver already mined and available in the vast slag heaps and tailings of Virginia and Gold Hill simply because it couldn't be profitably worked at the prevailing price of cartage to the stamp mills down on the Carson River!

Sharon reached for his stovepipe hat, threw an Inverness cloak around his shoulders and walked down C Street to the office of Wells Fargo &

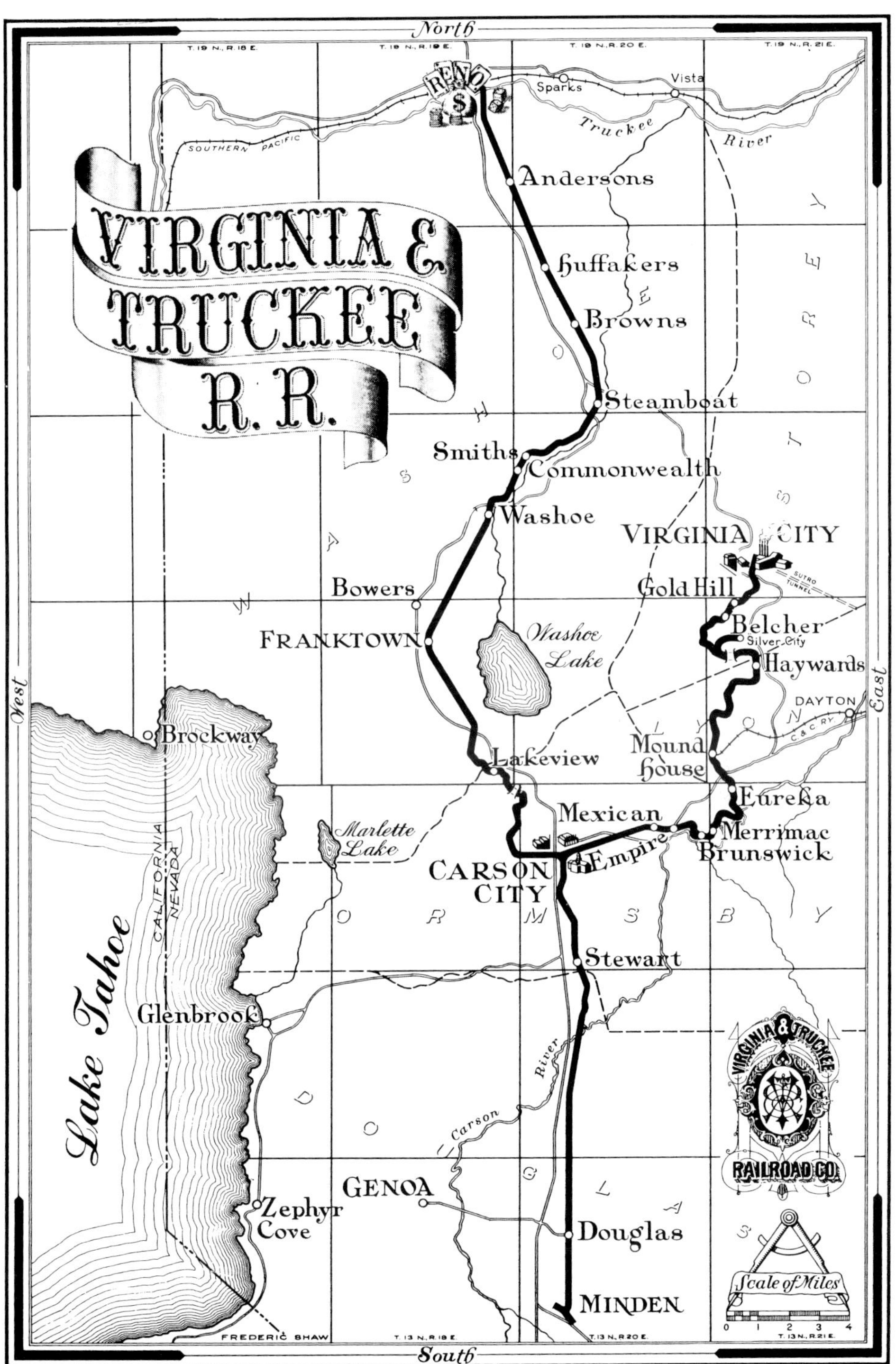

North
South
West
East
T. 19 N., R. 18 E.
T. 19 N., R. 19 E.
T. 19 N., R. 20 E.
T. 19 N., R. 21 E.
RENO
Sparks
Vista
Truckee River
SOUTHERN PACIFIC
VIRGINIA & TRUCKEE R.R.
Andersons
Huffakers
Browns
Steamboat
Smiths
Commonwealth
Washoe
VIRGINIA CITY
SUTRO TUNNEL
Gold Hill
Belcher
Silver City
Haywards
DAYTON
C. & C. RY.
Bowers
FRANKTOWN
Washoe Lake
Brockway
Lakeview
Mound House
Eureka
Mexican
Merrimac
Brunswick
Empire
Marlette Lake
CARSON CITY
CALIFORNIA
NEVADA
Lake Tahoe
Stewart
Glenbrook
Carson River
GENOA
Zephyr Cove
Douglas
MINDEN
STOREY
WASHOE
LYON
ORMSBY
DOUGLAS
VIRGINIA & TRUCKEE RAILROAD CO.
Scale of Miles
0 1 2 3 4
FREDERIC SHAW
T. 13 N., R. 18 E.
T. 13 N., R. 20 E.
T. 13 N., R. 21 E.

Co., where he booked passage on the next Pioneer Stage for Sacramento. He caught the night steamer *Antelope* there for San Francisco and three mornings later was closeted with Ralston and Mills in the latter's private office behind the impressive facade of the Bank of California.

All the rest of the United States, submitted Sharon with appropriate quotations from the classical humanities and Scripture to emphasize the need for speedy transport and communications, was building railroads. Their iron rails in various gages from the Erie's absurd six feet to the three-foot gage which General William Jackson Palmer was planning over in Colorado were being laid everywhere in a national orgy of finance that was almost a religion. Why in Tunket hadn't they thought of it before? What the Comstock needed was a railroad!

The amazing Central Pacific which had confounded critics who denounced it as "the Dutch Flat Swindle" by actually breasting the western approaches to the High Sierra would soon be running through the shacktown of Reno on its way to meet the Union Pacific at an as yet undetermined point, probably somewhere in Utah. The railroad, by Jupiter, Sharon swore, was the answer to the Bank of California's prayer, and with Mills' and Ralston's permission he would set about bringing one into being. All that had to be done was to locate a line from the Comstock down to the Carson River over which those hitherto unworkable ores could be cheaply transported and the most inaccessible shafts would be reopened. On the return trip up Sun Mountain the cars would carry timbers for the boilers and for shoring up the subterranean diggings themselves and would carry them at a rate which would overnight put an end to the monopoly of the teamsters and their exorbitant charges.

But, before this final move could be executed in Sharon's grand overall design for the acquisition of the wealth of the Comstock for the Bank of California, he was to undertake and accomplish one of the shrewdest financial coups of all the buccaneering saga of nineteenth century American finance. He set about acquiring for the Bank possession of all the reducing mills in the Nevada bonanzas. Most of these were in hard straits due to the declining production of the mines and, with infinite guile, Sharon allowed their owners to overextend themselves and write overdrafts against the Bank's Virginia branch until, turning on the mill owners with the ferocity of the grey wolf, he was able to foreclose on seven of the biggest mills on the banks of the Carson River. These were organized into the Union Mining and Milling Company, and, within two years were joined by ten lesser properties, so that by the year 1869 the Bank of California, without in any way involving itself in the speculative business of mining precious metals, a form of investment which met with the implacable disapproval of Mills, still had an absolute strangle hold on the mining industry in the Comstock. Without credit from the monopolistic bank, no mine in all the Comstock could operate, and unless its ores were reduced in the mills controlled by the bank there would, it was explained, be no credit forthcoming.

Then, and then only, did the Barons of the Bank of California allow themselves the pleasure of getting down to cases in the matter of their shrewdly conceived railroad.

Legend has it that Sharon sent for I. E. James, a surveyor of local note, and without preliminary discourse asked if he could locate a railroad from Virginia City to the Carson River. James, who had never run anything less conventional than a county boundary and a jerk-water road in the Midwest, ran a finger around the inside of his gates-ajar collar and weakly allowed that he guessed he could.

"Then do so at once," said Sharon, and that was that.

It was the original intention that the Virginia and Truckee should be but fifteen miles, more or less, in length, running from the mine shafts of the Comstock to the stamping mills along the Carson River, and to Dayton, and perhaps into Carson City, but with a functioning transcontinental railroad being built through Reno it would have been folly to neglect this opportunity for a mainline connection.

A charter for the project was already in the forethoughtful Sharon's pocket. The Nevada legislature had granted one to a group of promoters back in 1865 but their right to build had never been exercised and the charter was reissued as of March 5, 1868, and building started as soon as funds were in hand.

Although it was no conventional part of railroad financing in that day and age for promoters of railroads actually to invest their own funds in such speculative ventures, Sharon, Mills, and William Ralston diverged from the accepted pattern in such matters and tossed $1,500,000 of their own money into the project. Storey and Ormsby counties, through which the railroad would pass, issued bonds to the extent of half a million more, and the remaining independent mill owners ponied up with $387,000, some of it to be paid back in freight credits. Thus even the poor, struggling independents were finally rounded up by "the Bank crowd," although it must be said the arrangement was altogether to their advantage. Wood costs would be cut from $29 to $21 per thousand feet, almost a million a year would be saved over the amounts now paid to the teamsters, and the new low freight rates would allow the processing of the hitherto despised low grade ores. The setup was adrenalin to the whole pattern of the Comstock.

WELLS-FARGO MUSEUM

VIRGINIA & TRUCKEE RAILWAY

FOUNDING FATHERS OF THE V & T

Darius Ogden Mills, the greatest Western capitalist of his day (left) and one of the original three owners of the V & T, is shown here in a rare early photograph taken before he became the frosty titan of finance of the later nineteenth century. Beside him is Henry Yerington, the great General Superintendent of the V & T in its early decades. A former Carson mill owner, Yerington was persuaded to come along with the Bank of California in its construction and management of the V & T and was himself widely interested in lumber mills at Tahoe and other Nevada properties of importance. In an era of ornate personal appearance, his Chester A. Arthur mutton chop whiskers were the wonder and glory of the Washoe.

Surveyor James' location came to twenty-one miles into Carson City with a ruling grade of 2.2 per cent and a curvature equal to twenty-two full circles. The enemies of the Bank Triumvirate, who were not innumerous, had a basis in mathematical fact when they said the V & T was the crookedest railroad in the world. Grading started early in 1869 at American flat with 450 Chinese workmen, veterans of the Central Pacific's stormy construction days in the High Sierra and now released by that road's swift and easy progress down the Humboldt toward Promontory and glory. Fifteen construction camps were established and by early summer more than 1,600 workmen were spiking down the forty pound iron to untreated ties placed at intervals which would give a modern tracklayer the vapors. Picnic parties from Carson and Virginia used to drive out in buggies and carry-alls with basket lunches to watch the progress of the fabulous railroad, and the undertaking assumed overtones of festivity and hurrah as the spikes banged home, the coolies chattered like demented magpies and the long iron rails were run up across the desert in clouds of alkali dust by sweating teams and teamsters possessed of incendiary vocabularies.

The general superintendent of the V & T was Henry M. Yerington for whom, at a later date, the Nevada township which had previously been known as Pizen Switch changed its name. Yerington, possessor, in an age of universal beards, of what was generally admitted to be the finest set of sidewhiskers in the region, had originally been an independent mill owner who had been forced out by Sharon's squeeze play. Sharon knew him, however, for a man of unusual ability, and Yerington, who had too much sense to harbor a grudge, remained the ranking executive figure of the railroad until the time of his death many years later.

The railroad got under way with a whoop and a holler. September 28, 1869, was set as the day for Henry Yerington to drive a silver spike in the first rail to be laid in the shadow of Carson Mint, but when the editor of the *Appeal* appeared on the scene at the "painfully early" hour of seven which had been appointed, over his protest, as the great moment, he found that Yerington and James, unwilling to keep their track gangs idle for a single moment, had started the official proceedings half an hour earlier still. He was forced to fashion his account from the report of an interested eye witness. It was expected that rail would be laid at the rate of half a mile a day, but inside of a fortnight Yerington was laying a mile and a half daily and by October 3 the great Crown Point trestle at Gold Hill was actually completed.

Now the *Appeal* was full of railroad excitements. In one day it carried dispatches to the effect that the Central Pacific had rolled a train

ROY D. GRAVES

THE OLD TIMES LINGER AT CARSON

As late as 1938, with a cut of the J. G. Brill cars and other old timers in the foreground and excepting the oil fuel tank in the distance, the Carson yards of the V & T with their massive shops and engine house had changed little since the seventies. The track layout was much the same, the target switch stands were identical, and the Sierra eternal. On the page opposite at the top is the celebrated and superlatively beautiful wood burner, Genoa, shown at Carson in 1890. Below is No. 18, christened the Dayton, and outshopped by Central Pacific at Sacramento in 1874, and at the foot of the page is No. 20, the Tahoe, not too stylish of line in its latter years but still in service during the second World War on a foreign road in California.

CAPTAIN FREDERIC M. SHAW COLLECTION

W. A. PENNINGTON

G. M. BEST

through Reno with a single engine ahead of thirty-two cars, a new high in tonnage, that a vandal had attempted to burn the Central's trestle at Yuba; that the Salt Lake Branch Railroad was progressing nicely and that a great railroad banquet was being planned at Sacramento. A week later the cars were running between Carson and Empire and the editor of the *Appeal* was able to report that on an inspection run to the end of track "some ladies adorned the cowcatcher, the caboose was adorned by some of our fairest fair and we and some other handsome boys and girls sat on the tender."

"Our people spend all their holidays riding over the new track," said the paper and shortly afterward Yerington was forced to put a stop to these excursions in the interest of safety. " 'Bless me this is pleasant riding on the rail,' " the *Appeal* quoted editorially when it was possible to take the cars all the way to Mound House.

Two new locomotives from the East appeared on a siding at Reno with the letters "V C & T RR," and, since there was as yet no thought of running the iron except between Virginia and Carson the *Appeal* was forced to conclude the initials stood for "Virginia, Carson and Treadway," a local reference of humorous origin. The new road was generally spoken of as the Carson and Virginia and it was not until some months later that it was decided to extend it to a connection with the Central on the banks of the Truckee.

Almost from the very beginning, life for the V & T was positively a spasm of excitement. It was a railroad that was born rich, figuratively with a silver coal scoop on the deck of its locomotives, and its destiny was to be inextricably identified with champagne and balls and millionaires, with party dresses and picnics and junketings. Its passengers were to be the great and powerful and desirable folk of the world, all attracted to the inexhaustible Comstock and the fabled wonderments of Virginia City, a veritable Babylon precariously perched amidst the mineshafts and hoisting works above Six Mile Canyon.

The other two bonanza railroads of Nevada, the Eureka and Palisade and the Nevada Central off to the east in the White Pine and the Reese River countries, both came into being after the bonanzas they were built to serve had begun to decline, and their position in the world was not to be in any way comparable to the bright effulgence which shone about the Yankee Princess of all American railroads.

By the time the V & T was finished, the Comstock had been through its first great depression in 1865 and was within two years of the discovery of the incredible treasure which will forever be known as the Big Bonanza. So astounding was the wealth uncovered in the California and Consolidated Virginia mines that ever since that time historians have resorted to capitalization to differentiate this vast treasure from other and earlier discoveries along the Comstock. Times were good when the V & T was born; they were to become a cataclysm of wealth in its youth, and even in its maturity, until almost the very end, it was either to be tolerably self-supporting or else handsomely endowed and maintained by admirers.

Almost as soon as construction was under way reaching out toward Gold Hill and the Carson River in both directions from American Flat, Sharon had ordered two engines, the "Lyon" and the "Storey," and a third, the "Ormsby" was shortly afterward commanded. All were from Booth & Company and then a third order for the "Virginia" and the "Carson" was placed with the Baldwin works in the East. The three Booth locomotives were dismantled and hauled to Carson City, but the two Baldwins were scheduled to go into immediate service in construction work and were drawn by straining ox-team down through the Truckee Meadows as far as Steamboat Springs. Here, however, trouble was encountered, for the slim wooden bridge which sufficed for the buckboards of Wells Fargo & Company's pony express service out of Reno was too frail for the passage of these determined monsters, and they were forced to take the ford, to the detriment of pride and paint. Half way up the old Geiger Grade, not the smooth macadam auto road of today, but a far more exciting viastructure paralleling it which adventurous motorists who know of its existence can still take up the hill, the "Carson" was hopelessly bogged down in a pothole and had to be left for summer suns to dry it out. "Virginia" however at last rolled into the city of its name behind eighteen yoke of bellowing oxen and the saloons of C Street emptied themselves, and the balconies were crowded with cheering citizens as it hove into sight. Here was something even more wonderful and exciting than driving out to Mound House to watch the Chinese grading crews lay iron!

Two coaches, a mail car and baggage car were in the meantime being fabricated down at San Francisco, by the Kimball Manufacturing Company, while the V & T's first item of rolling stock, a little shanty car which later was to become the club car, "Julia Bulette," was being built right down at Carson yards by the railroad's mechanics.

It was at this period that the V & T began earning its reputation as the most champagne-conscious of all American railroads. Shrewd as he was in matters of finance, like his patron, William Ralston down in the Bank of California, Sharon admired to open wine when the occasion presented itself. A student of Shakespeare and the classical humanities and an orator of resounding periods, he was happiest when beguiling the public with entertainment of a major order and quoting from the Bard while the corks popped.

It was, therefore, no surprise to the happy citizenry when the arrival of the first train at Gold Hill, drawn by the little "Lyon" on November 12, 1869, was made the occasion for the first of a series of pleasant occasions, which were to continue throughout the entire lifetime of the railroad. The "Lyon" rolled in, an amazement of bunting, across the high Gold Hill trestle and with a great whooshing of exhaust from its enormous "Dolly Varden" stack, drew to a halt beside the red depot which may be seen to this day. There was beer in Mississippis for the general populace and vintage champagne, in enormous tubs of ice, for the distinguished guests. Whistles blew from every reducing mill and hoist all the way down the canyon to Silver City; the modest boiler pressure of the "Lyon" declined abruptly as the engineer leaned on the whistle cord; the people cheered and roared, the corks popped expensively and Sharon made spacious gestures to one and all to help themselves and to urge his neighbor to have more. It was all on the house.

Later, after appropriate welcomes had been expressed by the Mayor of Gold Hill and the editor of *The Gold Hill News* and after the Fire Department Band had rendered several selections, whose precise identity could only be surmised by reason of the booming of cannon from Fort Independence, Sharon unleashed the lightnings of oratory. He painted in lambent syllables the future of the Comstock, of which, indeed, who might speak with better authority? He pointed the way to illimitable vistas of opulence and power and to a future for Virginia City (and of course Gold Hill) beside which the dusty destinies of vanished Rome were of trifling consequence. When the V & T achieved the fullness of the operation for which it had been planned, the Comstock would tower fearfully and wonderfully, the ornament of the known and admiring world. None within hearing doubted the sentiments of the speaker for a moment, and everyone had another drink on the strength of them.

If the V & T was the glamor girl of American railroading, it may then fairly be said that its debutante party was Curry's Grand Fourth of July

THEN AND NOW: THE GLORY THAT WAS GOLD HILL

The upper photograph of Gold Hill facing The Divide was taken from a height above the southern end of the great V & T trestle at Crown Point. In the foreground are the hoisting works of the Yellow Jacket and in the middle foreground the populous city center with its residences, shops, mines, lumber yards and public buildings. Taken from the identical point three quarters of a century afterward, Gold Hill is a study in desolation. Of all its once countless structures only the deserted V & T depot in the left middle foreground and the hoisting works of the abandoned Yellow Jacket, right ditto, remain, and Gold Hill's only night life, where once the miners roared, is an all night public pay station of the telephone company.

GRAHAME HARDY COLLECTION

C. M. CLEGG

CARL WEEKS

SCENES AND SOUVENIRS OF THE SPACIOUS DAYS

Almost until the end, the V & T was a railroad celebrated for its excursions and here, behind No. 27 in Washoe Meadows opposite the Bowers Mansion, is a Nevada Day special rolling Carson-ward with an early snowfall already visible on the Sierra slopes. Across the page, at the top is the Reno, perhaps the most beloved of all V & T motive power, carrying stag horns and brass candlesticks on its great storm headlight coupled to a train of Kimball coaches in 1880. Reno was probably the most photographed, most familiarly known locomotive in the Old West for the many years of its picturesque and useful life. In the center is the switcher J. W. Bowker, property of the Pacific Coast Chapter of the Railroad and Locomotive Historical Society, as it appeared in the film "Union Pacific," and at the bottom is No. 22, the Inyo, a singularly stately engine entirely in the V & T tradition outshopped by Baldwin in 1875. Inyo is now the property of Paramount Pictures.

ROY D. GRAVES

G. M. BEST

DAVE WELCH

Railroad Ball with which the fine new shops at Carson were opened. For weeks in advance all Carson and Virginia, and of course, Gold Hill, Silver City, Genoa, Ophir, and Franktown were in a tizzy of excitement and the progress of the carpenters, the deliberations of the committee on arrangements and the details of the decoration occupied prominent space in the papers.

The enterprising Colonel Curry, who conceived the splendid idea, was reported to be paying $250.00 for the band, an astronomical sum in those pleasant times, and a gesture which would show even the nabobs of San Francisco what was what over the hill in Washoe. No fewer than 50,000 feet of three-inch planks were laid over the tracks and pits of the new shops and a bandstand erected in the center "no larger than a common house." Sorensen's Store supplied a hundred varicolored medallions for the walls and Japanese lanterns in uncounted numbers were swung from the beams, hoists and roof timbers. The walls of the shops themselves, as yet innocent of coalsmoke and grease, were whitewashed as clean "as new fallen snow" and a special coat of sizing applied to the height of a man's shoulder, that the whitewash might not come off on fragile evening gowns and stylish broadcloth.

"The Colonel has had every inch of dance floor nicely planed that the fantastic toe may encounter no slightest obstacle," reported the Carson *Appeal* in a vertigo of excited satisfaction, "and the entire idea approaches the confines of the sublime."

All Eagle Valley was outrageous with pride.

The night before the Fourth found Carson on the verge of dementia. Jacob Muller's Elegant Baths and Hair Dressing Salon was forced to stay open all night, so great was the press of custom. The *Appeal* announced that among those present on the morrow would be, in addition to the Governor and local dignitaries, both Sharon and the glittering William Ralston, prince of San Francisco banking, who would represent, according to the *Appeal,* "grand cash and broadgage capital." It was reliably reported that Perasich's San Francisco Market had imported six fresh pineapples to ornament the buffet, a gesture of uncommon spaciousness in the seventies when pineapples commanded five dollars gold at the shipside. The Fountain Restaurant was arranging an elaborate and satisfying buffet and the V & T had hauled to town a baggage car almost filled with cases of Louis Roderer champagne, the gift of the V & T's own William, later Senator, Sharon. The revels of imperial Rome knew no greater opulence!

The night of the ball itself the bars of Carson were treated to an elegance of attire unprecedented in the city's history. Silk hats and frock coats were the conventional attire of the time, but clawhammer evening coats and varnished boots from Roos Brothers in San Francisco were a comparative novelty at the Magnolia, Sarazac and Theater saloons and the genteel tap room of the Ormsby House.

And the attire of the fair sex which picked its way daintily across the rails of Carson yards to the V & T shops that unforgettable evening at eight o'clock to the minute, baffled the society reporters with its amazements of rich fabric and costly designs. To this day a gentle old lady of Carson remembers that her father had gone all the way to San Francisco for a Paisley shawl for her mother to wear on the night of nights, and she will show it to you.

A special train had brought down all the belles and eligible males of Virginia, whose ladies had spent the entire afternoon holding their hands above their heads, that their arms might achieve a fashionable degree of pallor.

Of the ball itself, the memory still lingers in the Nevada legend. Not even the Fourth of July roisterers who turned in a false alarm of fire at eleven o'clock, or the wretch who tossed a giant cracker through one of the south windows of the shops, were able to mar its brilliant progress. William Ralston showed up as promised. Sharon opened champagne in a manner to make the grand dukes of Russia, reportedly very extravagant fellows, look to their laurels. The revellers sat down to supper at the Fountain Restaurant's sumptuous buffet in relays of 150 at a time. There was lobster aspic and chicken salad and dainty watercress sandwiches and French vanilla ices and claret cup for the ladies, and a monsoon of champagne at Ralston's bar, over by the engine lathes. When the band had fiddled the last dollar's worth of waltz music (and everyone agreed it was a full $250's worth, too) and the last of the claret cup had been consumed, it was six o'clock and the sun was high in the heavens in the general direction of Dayton. Never, never would there be a fete comparable in grandeur, festivity and splendid moments to the great Fourth of July Ball of 1873!

By the time the V & T was a functioning reality, a decade after the first rush to the Comstock, Virginia City was no more of a wild and woolly community than, say, New York or San Francisco. It was, in point of terrain covered, and population, probably the richest city in the world and its manners, attire and traditions were those of the American West in an urban mood, but the overnight millionaires, the gunfighting in the streets and the prospecting of new claims were all in the past. Virginia society, conducted generally along the lines of that of San Francisco, was gay, formal and animated. The ladies of the Fair, Flood, Blauvelt, Mackay and King mansions, when they drove out in the afternoon, went in beautiful landaus and barouches behind blooded horses in silver trimmed harnesses. There were grand operas at Maguire's and Piper's, there were rich and cosmopolitan hotels, there was the world famed Washoe Club where visiting notables were wined and dined into a coma and whose furnishings, according to a reporter for Horace Greeley's *New York Tribune,* might well be the envy of nabobs in Fifth Avenue or Beacon Street.

In a midst where shop windows displayed merchandise which would have been deemed costly in the Rue de la Paix, and where champagne and evening dress were the veriest commonplace of daily life, the mine superintendents, bank managers, correspondents of San Francisco's commercial houses, and branch managers of stock brokerages, were men of wealth, dignity and importance, James Anson King, manager of Wells Fargo's banking branch at Virginia, lived high above A Street in a Victorian mansion which to this day shows traces of opulence and lavishness of taste which would have been considered ostentatious in Boston or Philadelphia. There were 150 saloons, six police stations and four churches. There were music halls, iron foundries and other great manufactories and there was a vast multiplicity of Chinese laundries and opium dens. All that Virginia needed to make it, not only indeed the Queen of the Comstock, but by far the most important city anywhere west of Chicago, and that included San Francisco, was a railroad.

For San Francisco was being built and financed by the Comstock. Its vast industrial enterprises, its seemingly impregnable Bank of California, its fantastic Palace Hotel, its cable cars, seaport and the Nob Hill mansions of its ever crescent colony of millionaires, were all being financed by the profits from Gould and Curry, Yellow Jacket, Ophir, Best and Belcher, Crown Point and the other fabled mines of Virginia, Gold Hill and Silver City.

By the time it was in full function, the V & T was serving not only the new Golconda, but the Paris of the western world.

No short line railroad in history was as familiar to the powerful, rich and celebrated of the world as was the V & T during the seventies and

THE KINGS ARE GONE: THE PALACES ARE DUST

In the mid-seventies at the time of the Big Bonanza, Virginia City was the opulent metropolis of the West. The V & T was serving a community of between 20,000 and 30,000 inhabitants and transients, and its gaudy wonderments, its millionaires and fabulous mines were lengendary throughout the world. Three quarters of a century later the V & T had gone from the Comstock, the city was populated by a handful of graying gaffers and in the distance only Sugar Loaf Mountain and Six Mile Canyon remained unchanged throughout the first coming and the final going of men.

ROBERT ALLEN COLLECTION

C. M. CLEGG

eighties. Hank Monk, the archetypal stage driver, was to achieve fame by terrifying Horace Greeley almost out of his whiskered wits, by taking him from Virginia to Placerville, over the breathless abysses of the King's Canyon Grade with six horses at a dead gallop, but the V & T got its passengers up to Gold Hill and Virginia in less strenuous manner.

At first the Comstock kings rode more or less informally in long cabooses with facing longitudinal benches and a row of magnificent cuspidors "of tasteful and fanciful pattern" ranged down the middle of their aisles. Then came the beautiful coaches and combines built in one of William Ralston's carriage shops in San Francisco, with elaborately decorated oilcloth ceilings and red velour seats and little curlycue baggage racks, which could accommodate nothing more voluminous than a small brief case. One of these was, until a short while since and may still be, in the coach house of the Bath and Hammondsport, in upstate New York where it was stored after appearing in "Railroads on Parade" at the New York World's Fair of fragrant memory.

The Central Pacific was reluctant to allow its costly Silver Palace sleeping cars run over the V & T's precipitous grades, and the high trestle at Gold Hill, until one fine morning in the early seventies, the celebrated car "Pullman" with its designer on board came up to Virginia on the end of the night train from Reno, after which demonstration of faith the Central relaxed and sleepers were put into regular operation out of San Francisco.

And after the sleepers, inevitably, came the golden age of private railroad cars bearing the great, and assistant great, to behold at first hand the wonders of the Yellow Jacket and Cholar-Potosi, to perform on the stage of Piper's Opera House or to attend stupefying banquets in their honor, at the Washoe Club or the International Hotel. In this manner came President Grant and General Sherman and Governor Leland Stanford of California aboard his ornate car, "The Stanford," which had pleasantly outraged public opinion by costing $30,000, when his wife gave it to him as a birthday present. By the time he was United States Senator, Sharon too had a private car and it was, of course, frequently taken up from Carson Yards with, it may be imagined, a deal of careful handling and gentle spotting on the house track at Virginia.

LUXURY OF A VANISHED ERA

This interior, of one of the Detroit coaches built for the V & T in 1874, shows in detail the plush seats, oil lamps, conductor's desk and beautifully painted oilcloth ceilings characteristic of the coach-builder's art at this period.

ROY D. GRAVES

The Emperor Dom Pedro of Brazil unhappily bypassed Virginia City, although he wanted to see the Bear River trestle of the Nevada County Narrow Gage over in California, but Phineas Barnum brought notables to Virginia in a tumult of publicity, and was followed in their private Pullmans and Silver Palace sleepers, by Helena Modjeska, Adelina Patti, John McCullough, Ada Isaacs Menken, Salvini the Younger, Edwin Booth and Maude Adams. David Belasco, who was stage manager at Piper's in the early days, used to ride it regularly and, of course, all of the executives of the Bank of California, and later the Bank of Nevada, had drawing rooms aboard its overnight sleepers from Oakland Mole.

When the party of the Baron Rothschild arrived in an uncommonly beautiful private car, Yerington was so enchanted by its style and decor that he was able to persuade Darius Mills that a man of his position could scarcely afford to ride in common Pullmans, and that he, too, should have a private car. Mills, always conservative, balked at paying the Pullman works the $35,000 which was their estimate on such a vehicle, and thriftly instructed Yerington to rebuild one of the V & T's passenger coaches as his private hack. This Yerington was able to accomplish in the Carson shops at the bargain rate of $2,500 and Mills, down in San Francisco, at once set about preparations for a stylish trip to Washington. Yerington was charged with the task of finding a good cook, but it seems that Clarence Mackay saw the car and somehow contrived to borrow it before even the V & T's president was able to set foot aboard his own property. Whether or not he ever took it to Washington isn't in the record. Yerington was inordinately pleased with the car and himself travelled widely in it under the liberal arrangements for such de luxe voyaging which obtained at the times, and maintained that it was a fine advertisement for the V & T.

He was also forever writing friends about the splendors of this paradigm of all luxurious varnish, and more than once his letters to friends and business associates casually mentioned the circumstance that "my car is now in the East being occupied by his family and Mr. John Mackay, one of the Bonanza Kings and the richest man in the world."

Ever a great railroad for picnics, excursions and jollifications, the V & T was constantly being called on for special trains to take the Brigade Nevada Militia for a state review by the Governor at Carson or to transport the Turnverein for a picnic in Washoe Meadows at the Sandy Bowers Mansion where there were swimming pools, shade trees and other conveniences for relaxation and philosophy.

The Bowers Mansion, a stately pile of Victorian solidity, erected by one of the Comstock pioneers endowed with more luck than sagacity and maintained by his widow, Eiley Orrum, the "Washoe Seeress," as a

NEVADA STATE MUSEUM

THE CLASSIC POSE IN OLD VIRGINIA CITY

In 1905 the graceful engine Reno, No. 11, was converted to burn oil and here it is with its crew, Coonie Pohl, engineer, and Jim Savage, fireman, posed in the yards at Virginia City. Below is No. 12, the Genoa, photographed outside the Virginia depot, probably about 1890, with a fine assortment of bowler hats and the railfans of the period in evidence in the foreground.

CAPTAIN FREDERIC M. SHAW COLLECTION

pleasure resort, is now a county museum. It had, then as now, wide terraces, spacious lawns and agreeable vistas and was a favorite of the miners in their more pastoral moods. The Widow Bowers, who had been to call on the Queen of England, although not exactly received (Washoe never did learn the precise details) was accustomed to receive them in her front parlor amidst relics of more solvent splendor until their exhilaration achieved the gun-firing stage, when she would retire to her private apartments and appear no more until the last reveller had been carried to the waiting cars down in the meadows.

There were, to be sure, minor tumults and uproars within the family circle of the V & T during its early years. In 1875 Yerington found occasion to purchase from the Baldwin works two switchers, one of which, the "J. W. Bowker," is still preserved, the property of the Pacific Coast chapter of the Railway and Locomotive Historical Society. "The switch engine for Carson I shall name 'The James,'" Yerington wrote to Mills, "and the Virginia switcher I would like to name 'The J. W. Bowker' after our master mechanic as it would please the old man."

Less than six months after this Bowker was out of favor with the general superintendent. It would seem that the old sir had long been possessed of a leaning for the bottle and one afternoon the shops were disturbed by a fearful row between Bowker and his foreman and, when it was ascertained by Yerington that his master mechanic was, as he later wrote Mills, "full up of whisky," he was summarily discharged.

There was nothing, it would appear, small about Bowker's skirmishes with strong waters for, a month from the day of his discharge, Yerington wrote his employer that the once valued employee was still in his cups, rolling through the taverns of Virginia and complaining of his treatment by the V & T to interested loungers in the Crystal Chandeliers and the Sazarac. He even threatened the railroad, claiming that he had not been paid for a smokestack he had installed in its locomotives and to which he owned the patent, but nothing came of it and in time Bowker seemed to have disappeared from the C Street scene.

A perpetual thorn in Yerington's side and what he chose to regard as his cross in life was James G. Fair, one of the celebrated Bonanza Kings of the Comstock, who was always at loggerheads with the V & T's general manager. Yerington might be on the best of terms with Flood and O'Brien, the millionaire saloon keepers, and might loan his elegant private car to Mackay, but with Fair there was nothing but trouble.

Mostly the arguments were over rates on bringing in lumber for the furnaces of Fair's great stamping mills along the Carson and timber for the stopes and wintzes of his mines up the hill at Virginia. In January, 1876, things had reached such an impasse between the mine king and the railroad that Fair resorted to threats to gain his ends. He remarked to Isaac Requa, superintendent of the Comet Mine, that he was contemplating building a narrow gage railroad of his own from Virginia directly over the hill to Reno and did he, Requa, know of a good surveyor? Fair knew perfectly well that the best surveyor in the Comstock was Ike James who had located the V & T, but he also knew that Requa was a confirmed gossip in the saloons of C Street and that the matter would be in Yerington's ear before the day was out.

In this he was right and Yerington, in a great tizzy, was shortly writing Mills the shocking news and asking what, in this dire pass, he was to do?

Before he could hear from San Francisco, Yerington encountered Fair in the street and bluntly accused him of attempting to blackmail his way to lower rates with talk of a railroad he never seriously contemplated. Fair took no exception to Yerington's language but told him that he would act in the matter as soon as he knew Mills' mind. Apparently a compromise was agreed upon for there was no more talk of a narrow gage down the Geiger Grade or by any other route to Reno.

A great deal has been written about the frontier journalism of the old West, underscoring its integrity and the homely virtues of honesty and fearlessness on the part of its editors, but there is reason to believe that these existed more in the fancy of historians than in recorded fact. A case in point is the long catalogue of villification and abuse to which the V & T and its owners were subjected by Denis McCarty, editor of the *Virginia Chronicle.* Under McCarty, the *Chronicle* was little more than a large scale blackmail operation and its abuse of the V & T was solely dictated by the hope that Mills and Sharon would tire of its nuisance value and buy out McCarty who named the fantastic sum of $50,000 as its price. When, a few years after, the *Chronicle* did indeed close, its assets were sold for less than $500.

Yerington, in his capacity as spokesman for Mills, offered McCarty a salary of $150 monthly to call off his editorial dogs, but McCarty sent down word to Carson that he couldn't accept a retainer of this sort but was quite agreeable to the equivalent in advertising from the mines associated with the V & T and for passes for himself and his staff over the road itself.

Upon receipt of this intelligence Yerington, his whiskers and coat-tails standing out in the slipstream, jumped on a light engine then standing in Carson yards, and hastened up the hill to conclude negotiations. There could be no doubt that McCarty had gotten under everybody's corporate skin. The next day Yerington was able to write Mills that

T. G. WURM

T. G. WURM

LUCIUS BEEBE

CAPTAIN FREDERIC M. SHAW COLLECTION

UGLY DUCKLINGS OF THE ROUND HOUSE

Not all the V & T's motive power over its eighty years of operations could be described as either ornamental or successful. Above is the unfortunate engine known as "First No. 25" which Superintendent Yerington acquired from the Union Pacific. Despite its handsome lines, its frame was so rigid that on its first run it broke a dismaying number of rails between Carson and Virginia, and Yerington smuggled it out of town in disgrace and in dead of night. On the page opposite are shown three other V & T orphans. At the top is a motor railbus which, for a time during the thirties, was placed on the run between Carson and Virginia. Below it is an even less beautiful rail car, No. 99, which was bought in 1917 and boasted a White automobile motor and a makeshift chassis by Thomson-Graf-Edler of San Francisco. At the bottom is the McKeen gasoline car which for several years spent more time in the shops than in service and was a trial to all concerned. It now serves as a restaurant in Carson City.

"McCarty has come to terms for $150 advertising per month and the passes and agrees to wheel into line, quit his abuse of you and act like a white man from now on."

Even Wells Drury in his *An Editor on the Comstock Lode* never finds occasion to mention Denis McCarty's business ethics.

In its hour of greatness the V & T was a veritable paradigm of successful railroad operation and management, and officials from other roads arrived in ornate business cars in numbers to interview Yerington in the general manager's office at Carson and ride the grades above Empire. They inspected the fortress-like shops and engine house in Carson Yards, marveled at the Gold Hill trestle towering above the hoists of the Yellow Jacket and were wined into happy comas by Sharon in the world-famous Washoe Club at Virginia amidst surroundings and art objects that were the envy of millionaires in Fifth Avenue and on Nob Hill. The V & T was by way of becoming a legend along with the Comstock it served.

In eighty years the fundamentals of its operation were never changed. Trains were dispatched by telegraphic order, later by telephone. Its stub switches, target switch stands and light rail from the mills of Sheffield, are still in useful operation. Its locomotives, first burning wood, later coal and still later oil fuel, were always of traditional steam design. No diesel ever rolled over its right of way although, at one time, and with a notable lack of effectiveness, passengers were carried in a McKeen gasoline motor coach. This unsightly herdic, painted a bright red, and with portholes for windows, spent most of its time in the shops and now is a lunch wagon on the outskirts of Carson. Even as a dog wagon it was no great success and has several times changed hands.

The operating life of the V & T over the eight decades of its existence was singularly free from the melodrama and catastrophe so often associated with mountain railroading in the old West. There never was a serious wreck and never a really important train robbery. Wells Fargo's armed messengers rode the bright yellow combines and treasure cars with but few occasions to burn black powder in the interest of property protection. The great trestle at Gold Hill, the road's greatest potential for calamity, never was the scene of an accident and although tunnels burned out and there were occasional derailments, the Nevada press was hard put to read dramatic overtones into these incidents of operation in an age when, elsewhere, train wrecks were of monstrous proportions. Operating speed on the grades north of Carson were extremely conservative, the equipment was scrupulously maintained in the great shops at that point and over most of the line there was a high order of visibility.

In the natural course of events, tramps, Chinamen and livestock were annihilated and drunks who chose the rails for a couch came to no good end, but the most sensational headlines the *Enterprise* could evolve were "Death of a Vagrant Beneath the Wheels" or "A Tragedy in Chinatown" when some bemused Celestial in a poppied coma fell in front of the night sleeper. Romance rode the V & T but it was the romance of riches and not of violence.

By 1873, according to Gilbert Kneiss, a ranking historian of nineteenth century railroading in the American West, Mills, Ralston and Sharon were sharing a cool $100,000 monthly profit from the railroad, but almost everyone connected with the V & T seemed to share in its own splendid bonanza. That the golden harvest was not confined to the nabobs of Virginia and San Francisco is attested by the record which shows that in the middle seventies the road's section foreman at Franktown, where the Flying ME Ranch now stands adjacent to the track, was murdered for the sum of $6,000 he was known to have about his person. Few section foremen of other railroads have been possessed of such sums.

Throughout the seventies after the uncovery of the Big Bonanza, as the last fabulous treasure of the Comstock came to be known, excitement piled upon excitement for the V & T. Motive power was in constant requisition, and the rail fans of the period, who included almost every member of the populace in any American community, were able to admire the acquisition of four more Baldwins in 1875 alone, while the previous year three Baldwins and two Cooke engines were added to the ever growing roster of Yerington's motive power.

In the middle of the decade the cataclysmic collapse of the Bank of California ended with the death of the brilliant Ralston who, only a few days before the closing of its doors, had sold his share of the V & T to Mills in an effort to bolster the Bank's tottering destinies. From then on the profits, still so great that, as Kneiss recounts, the staff was accustomed to sit up all night at the Virginia offices counting the day's take in gold double eagles, were divided between Sharon and Mills on a one-third, two-thirds basis.

By 1879 the mines were again beginning to show a decline and, although they continued to be profitable for another two decades, the real glory of the Comstock was fading. In 1879, too, President Grant aboard his private car "California" was brought to Virginia to be stupefied with hospitality, overwhelmed with oratory and dined into a splendid stupor amidst the decanters and Victorian cruet sets which adorned the tables of the International Hotel. It took a stout constitution at any time to withstand Comstock entertainment and for a past President of the United States, chefs and bartenders, toastmasters and cellarmen went into a special trance and brought forth sybaritic follies of monstrous proportions.

In 1880, when the pattern of Nevada mining was spreading to the southward and overflowing across the state boundary in Mono County in California, there came into being, with capitalization of Mills and Sharon behind it and Henry Yerington as its manager, one of the most remote little railroads in all the record of the old West. The narrow gage Carson and Colorado was built to connect the then booming mining towns of Hawthorne, Candelaria, Bodie, Aurora and Benton with the V & T at Mound House five miles east of Carson City and it was originally planned to run it to the Colorado River. But construction was halted at Keeler near Owens Lake in the shadow of Mount Whitney and there a portion of it has remained until this day as the Owens Valley branch of the Southern Pacific and the only narrow gage trackage of this mighty carrier.

Neither of the wicked towns of Aurora and Bodie were to be included in the C & C trackage but were to be connected by a short line running from Benton and known as the Bodie and Benton. Although the B & B eventually materialized it never did get as far as Benton, but it has survived in the Western legend on the basis of its little engines, "Mono," "Inyo" and "Tybo." A wag of the time remarked that when its finances were improved the road would "probably acquire three or fomo."

In a way the southern branch of the V & T which eventually came to be known as the Carson & Colorado (in the beginning Yerington wanted to call it the Nevada Southern) was a tribute to Sharon's unquenchable enthusiasm for mining ventures and in another to his foresight in suppressing competition. It was Sharon who proposed that it be narrow gaged and it was Sharon, through Yerington's agency, who finally overcame Mills' reluctance to expand the V & T system beyond its then dimensions. Promises of economy and the rumored threat of a rival railroad to be built into the rich Esmeralda diggings of Bodie and Aurora finally persuaded Mills. Yerington arranged with the unions for the grading to be done by white labor to Dayton and by Chinese from Dayton south. "If the entire line had to be graded by white labor I would not think of driving a pick into the ground," wrote Yerington, "but would abandon the undertaking entirely." For its grading Yerington himself perfected a "wheeled scraper" to be operated by two horses and one man which may well have been the lineal ancestor of the bulldozer of modern usage. A trusy agent was dispatched into the High Sierra to note the performance of engines of the Nevada County Narrow Gage.

But the C & C never really won Mills' affection and legend has it that when Sharon and Yerington took him on a dusty two days' inspection trip over the newly completed little 293-mile pike, the huffy financier shook his head and was gloomily of the opinion that "they had built the railroad either 300 miles too long, or 300 years too soon."

COURTESY DR. J. E. WIER: NEV. STATE HIST. SOC.

THE DESERT RECLAIMS ITS OWN

Mound House at the turn of the century was a busy transfer point for freight and passengers and the northern terminal of the narrow gage Carson and Colorado. Here freight was transshipped to standard gage cars on the V & T whose main line to Virginia City is visible in the upper photograph. Seen from the identical spot today, the place that was Mound House is a desert wasteland with only rotting ties and a single decaying shack to show where once thriving railroads ran.

C. M. CLEGG

LUCIUS BEEBE

NARROW GAGE SOUVENIR OF YESTERDAY

Once the Carson and Colorado was the hopefully financed narrow gage subsidiary of the V & T and ran from Mound House to Keeler, California, by way of Mount Montgomery Pass and a number of promising mining camps. Today only seventy miles of its track running from Keeler to Laws survive as the only narrow gage branch of the great Southern Pacific with freight service three times a week over its entire mileage. Here is three-foot-gage No. 18 with an extra water tank and a solitary, diminutive combine, now in service as a way car, running through the beautiful countryside near its northern terminus at Laws. The V & T sold the C & C at the turn of the century and its Nevada trackage was abandoned thirty years or so later.

For many years this dark prophecy seemed vindicated and the road remained an orphan among Nevada railroads. Many of the southern mines failed of their original rich promise although both Aurora and Candelaria continued to produce fitfully right into the twentieth century. Some borax was hauled out from the Keeler end, but the road was continually in borrasca and in 1900 Mills sold it in its entirety to the Southern Pacific which continued to operate it as the Nevada & California Railroad.

It was only after its disassociation with the V & T that good times came to the Carson & Colorado. The Tonopah and Goldfield booms blossomed into bonanzas of incalculable richness and Jim Butler's errant burro, in whose pursuit its owner made the first Tonopah strike, had started a stampede that was to bring thousands of adventurers to the southern desert. More than $125,000,000 was to come out of the diggings at Tonopah alone, and Marsh and Stimler's discoveries a year or so later at Goldfield were to create a new generation of millionaires of which George Nixon and George Wingfield were the Nevada representatives while outsiders such as Montana's acquisitive Senator Clark and New York's Bernard Baruch and Charles M. Schwab were to take hundreds of thousands of dollars of Nevada wealth out of the state.

In the early years of Tonopah the nearest rail connection was with the Carson and Colorado at Mina and until the completion of the Tonopah Railroad all ore was freighted out to the railroad by team. These were indeed blue days and fair for the orphaned and rejected little Carson and Colorado and in a single year it repaid its purchase price of $2,750,000 to the Southern Pacific. Its diminutive combines and passenger coaches bulged with mining engineers, prospectors, eastern capitalists, adventurers, gamblers, strumpets, gunmen and music hall troupes, and northbound ore cars sagged with unaccustomed consignments of rich freight, some of which assayed as high as $579,000 for a forty-eight ton carload.

The Nevada desert bloomed with gold and guns and girls and between its connection at Reno and its Carson and Colorado terminus at Mound House, the Southern Pacific was bringing a vast revival of business to the V & T. Memories of the Comstock times were evoked as entire trainloads of mining machinery, foodstuffs, building materials, roulette wheels, mahogany bars and all the integral parts of mining civilization rolled through Truckee Meadows to clog the yards at Mound House so that shipments were often delayed a month or more at this bottleneck. Simply, the Carson and Colorado didn't have the rolling stock to take over what was consigned to it by the V & T. In the end, the Southern Pacific, not entirely pleased with putting money in the pocket of a line which did no more than link two of its own properties, built the Hazen branch of its own rails connecting with the Tonopah and Goldfield at Mina and by-passing the V & T altogether. The last V & T boom ended, as had the others before it, in the inevitable decline into borrasca. Today only the ninety miles of narrow gage between Keeler and Laws, California, survive as vestigial traces of the little Carson and Colorado and on the truck plates of its one remaining combine, now used as a way car, may be traced to the inscription indicative of its origins long ago: The letters read "V & T RR, Carson."

In an oblique manner, too, the V & T and the Comstock itself participated in the last great bonanza in the southern desert. In 1904 the vast Butters reducing mill employing more than 300 workmen was built in Six Mile Canyon, a costly monument to the optimism of the Comstock even though its mines were almost at the final end of their resources. When the strike at Tonopah came in, this was the nearest place its ores could be worked and the fabulous ores of the Jumbo and Mohawk mines were for a time carried in wagon freight to Mina where they were shipped to Mound House over the Carson and Colorado and thence up the grade to Virginia City over the V & T. A branch was built down the precipitous descent into Six Mile Canyon and the ore, in a curious reversal of traffic, was processed at Butters plant. In a year or two, however, Tonopah had its own mills, and today no trace of the V & T spur remains and the tremendous mills it served are but a heap of rubble amidst concrete emplacements.

Railroad historians have, from time immemorial, been fascinated by the literal disappearance of locomotives from the railroads they served, much as though they might be mislaid like the proverbial plumber's tools. The V & T at one time had a mystery locomotive generally known as "First No. 25," a stylish American type eight wheeler acquired second hand from the Union Pacific back in 1902. Almost as soon as it was put in commission, No. 25 disappeared into what amounted to thin air and no amount of enquiry for its whereabouts produced a satisfactory answer. Indeed, Superintendent Yerington was remarked to become irritated at its merest mention. The truth was that First No. 25 was so rigid of frame that on its initial run it broke no fewer than nineteen rails on the sharp curves in the hills between Carson and Virginia and that, enraged by this lapse from decorum, Yerington had, secretly and in dead of night, sneaked it out of town and sold it down the river to Towle Brothers Lumber Company at Emigrant Gap. Shortly after this a second No. 25 appeared on the motive power roster and remained in service until 1947 when it, in turn, was sold south, this time to the film studios of Hollywood. Yerington was no man to admit an error in judgment on

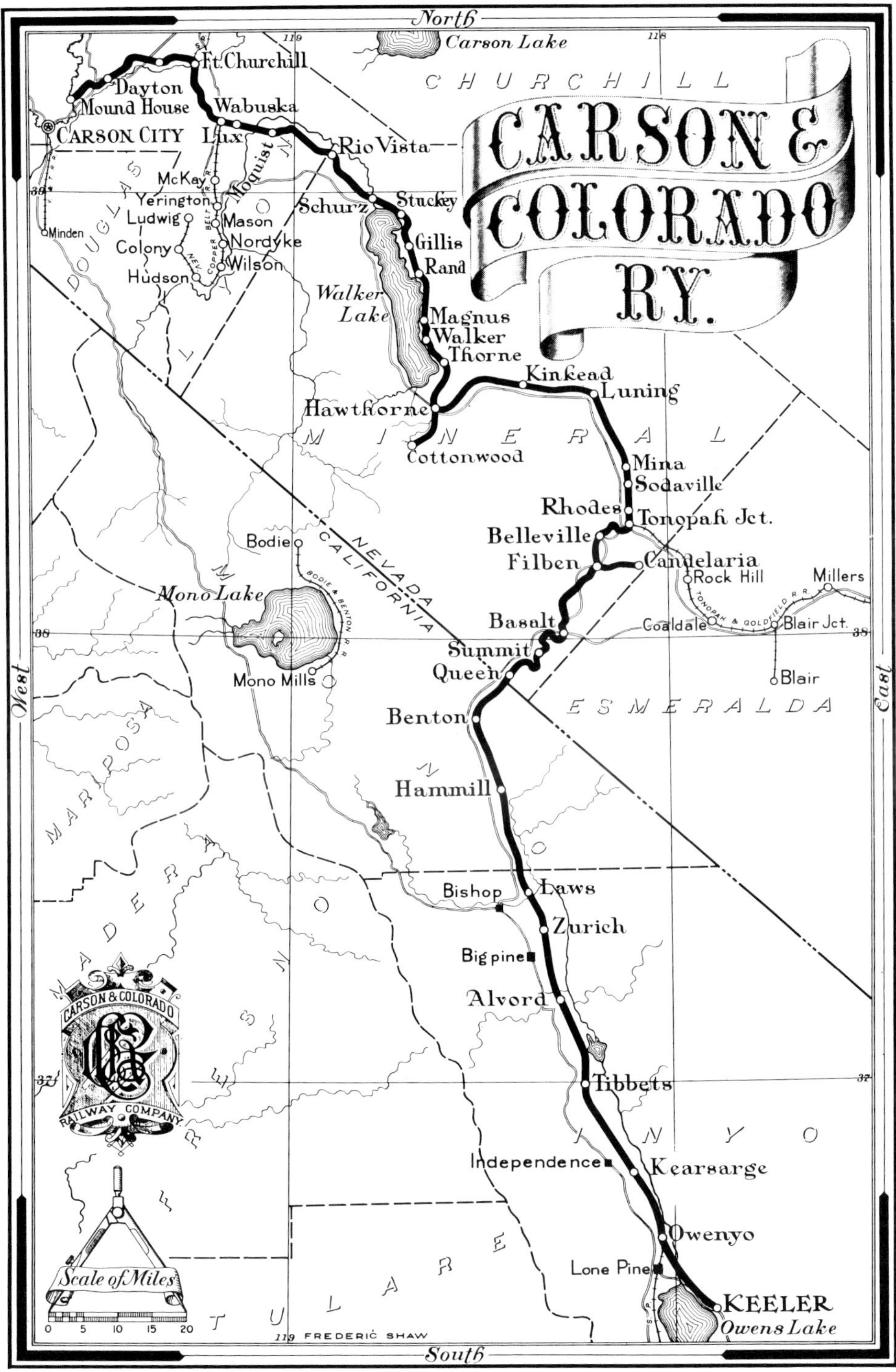

North
South
West
East
CARSON & COLORADO RY.
Carson Lake
CHURCHILL
Ft. Churchill
Dayton
Mound House
CARSON CITY
Wabuska
Lux
Moquist
Rio Vista
McKay
Yerington
Ludwig
Mason
Nordyke
Colony
Wilson
Hudson
Minden
DOUGLAS
LYON
Schurz
Stuckey
Gillis
Rand
Walker Lake
Magnus
Walker
Thorne
Hawthorne
Cottonwood
Kinkead
Luning
MINERAL
Mina
Sodaville
Rhodes
Tonopah Jct.
Belleville
Filben
Candelaria
Rock Hill
Millers
TONOPAH & GOLDFIELD R.R.
Coaldale
Blair Jct.
Blair
Basalt
Summit
Queen
Benton
ESMERALDA
NEVADA
CALIFORNIA
Bodie
BODIE & BENTON R.R.
Mono Lake
Mono Mills
MONO
MARIPOSA
MADERA
FRESNO
Hammill
Bishop
Laws
Zurich
Big pine
Alvord
Tibbets
INYO
Independence
Kearsarge
Owenyo
Lone Pine
KEELER
Owens Lake
TULARE
CARSON & COLORADO RAILWAY COMPANY
Scale of Miles
0 5 10 15 20
FREDERIC SHAW
119
118
38
37

LUCIUS BEEBE

ALL, ALL ARE GONE, THE OLD FAMILIAR FACES"

In the summer of 1948, No. 27, which had been built by Baldwin in 1913, was retired and is shown here on its last run working steam a mile or so north of Steamboat, a gallant and graceful locomotive to the end. On the page opposite are some now vanished examples of V & T passenger equipment. At the top is one of the handsome wooden coaches with arched transoms of colored glass above their windows in service until 1947 when it was sold to Hollywood. In the center is one of the passenger carrying cabooses built by Kimball in San Francisco in 1872, now the property of Paramount Pictures. In 1939 it made a 12,000 mile tour of the United States as part of the promotion for the film "Union Pacific" in the preparation of which one of the authors of this book was associated with Cecil B. DeMille as technical director. At the bottom is the club car, Julia Bulette, rebuilt in the last years of the V & T from its first piece of rolling stock which had been constructed in 1869 at Carson as a way car.

LUCIUS BEEBE

G. M. BEST

LUCIUS BEEBE

the part of Henry Yerington, but the midnight disappearance of rolling stock from the V & T wasn't unique with No. 25. Almost half a century later the little club car "Julia Bulette" and two fine old wooden coaches vanished from service without public mention of their going and turned up, to the surprise of nobody, in the studios of Hollywood.

March 17, 1897, was to witness a positive vertigo of excitements for the V & T. The Corbett-Fitzsimmons championship box fight was scheduled to take place at Carson and the world of sports and fashion descended upon the sleepy Nevada countryside in thousands. In anticipation of this happy event the V & T notified all the mills of the Comstock that the transportation of heavy freight for the mines would be suspended for a week. Every locomotive in the Carson roundhouse was fired up and kept in almost constant operation for that period with specials, excursions and private cars of fearful and wonderful decor and opulent resources of whisky and champagne in their ice boxes. Empty coaches clogged half the sidings between Carson and Reno and sleepers and diners and other luxury rolling stock were spotted in seemingly endless profusion under the tall cottonwoods in Carson yards.

The Southern Pacific's chief dispatcher at Ogden reported no fewer than thirty special trains of solid Pullmans through from the East the day before the fight. The V & T hauled a special of ten Pullmans from Los Angeles alone and nine Wagner Palace cars from Cincinnati. Senator David Ingalls of Kansas, who, oddly enough, was reporting the doings for the New York *Journal,* arrived in a private car, as did Charlie Clark, son of Montana's affluent and acquisitive senior senator, who had borrowed his father's private car for the occasion and arrived with a party of "dead game sports in purple and fine linen with well groomed tiles." The report that the private hack boasted a marble bathtub and gold plumbing fixtures attracted crowds of curious who gazed in awe at its gold scrollwork and gleaming brass rails.

All in all, the strain on the V & T's resources was even greater than it had been back in the crisis caused by the big fire up at Virginia in '75, but somehow the tracks and trestles stood up under more than a hundred special trains, mostly Pullmans, and after the fight the *San Francisco Examiner* had the entire right of way to Reno cleared for its own press special which raced to its Southern Pacific connection with a number of staff artists and photographers on board including Homer Davenport who had been engaged to chronicle the fight of the century. Private cars were to roll over the V & T in later years but never in such florid profusion as they did that windy spring of 1897.

It is interesting to note that even the little Carson and Colorado shared in the general excitement since almost the entire population of Bodie, Aurora and Candelaria demanded transport to the fight and many of

LUCIUS BEEBE

SMOKE AND GLORY IN THE GRAND MANNER

This double header in the Minden meadows shows Nos. 25 and 26 running in tandem with a mixed consist including the club car, Julia Bulette. The train was specially made up and run for the authors of this book by Gordon Sampson, General Manager of the V & T, and provided a fine record of old time motive power and rolling stock which can never again be assembled.

them made it in boxcars converted into club cars by the simple placing of a board between two barrels and installing a bartender. The C & C's few coaches and diminutive combines could never have accommodated the determined miners who finally arrived at Mound House in a pleasant alcoholic tumult and were taken over there by the V & T. The Bodie contingent had had to dig a road through the snow in all-night shifts to get to the narrow gage at Benton.

So far as the record shows the only private car, other than one built by Yerington in the Carson shops for Darius Mills back in the '70's to claim the V & T as its home railroad was the last such varnish ever to roll over the Carson meadows and up the ruling grade at Lakeview. It was "The Gold Coast," property of the authors of this monograph, which came to the V & T and was spotted for the summer under the cottonwoods in Carson yards. They had purchased the venerable hack from the Georgia Northern where it had served as business car for the road's president after seeing service in a similar capacity on the Live Oak, Perry and Gulf in Florida, where it had often been drawn through the swamps and along the bayous by graceful, balloon stacked wood burners. In the twilight of the V & T's years "The Gold Coast" brought to Carson a final touch of the luxury which had characterized the railroad's salad days, and the laughter of gracious guests and the popping of wine corks echoed for the last time across the midnight yards.

"The Gold Coast" had an added sentimental value for old timers in Nevada. Its interior decor was evolved by a Hollywood decorator to recreate the Victorian drawing room and dining salon of "The Stanford," the private car of Governor Leland Stanford, first president of the Central Pacific Railroad. The 1870 palace car, the gift to her husband of Mrs. Stanford, was for more than three decades an institution in the old West and upon occasion had been run over the V & T with visiting notables aboard. Three quarters of a century later, "The Gold Coast" fulfilled a similar agreeable function and Governor Vail Pittman and other notables were entertained in its Victorian apartments.

After the epic convulsions of the nineteenth century the V & T enjoyed briefly the heady excitements of the southern Nevada bonanzas as long as they lasted, and then settled into four long decades of genteel poverty and decline. In 1906 it was extended fifteen miles past the Indian reservation and town at Stewart down the richly cultivated Carson Valley to Minden. Minden, famous for its lamb and beef, butter and other wealthy dairy products, gradually became the major point of origin of its freight as the mills along the Carson River shut down and the mines at Virginia closed for the last time. In 1938 the rails between Car-

C. M. CLEGG

V & T VIGNETTES: 1948

The celebrated V & T depot and general offices at Carson, shared by a stage station and shaded by cottonwoods and Lombardy poplars. Below, in a very mixed train indeed, in the depot at Carson is the car "The Gold Coast," property of the authors of this monograph. It was aboard this reminder of upholstered Edwardian times that they prepared the material for this and other Western history matters, and it is shown here, headed for San Francisco, behind the V & T's passenger combine, United States Railway Post Office and a mixed consist of tanks and high cars ready to pull out of Carson at sunset.

ACME NEWSPHOTOS

son City and Virginia were torn up and the railroad's great days became only a memory.

The year before that, Ogden Mills, who had inherited the property from his grandfather and purchased the outstanding shares from the Sharon estate on a basis of sentiment, died suddenly. He had paid its annual deficits out of pocket, being a very wealthy man, as a matter of family pride, but no provision had been made for its future. His obituaries in the newspapers of the land were in effect the handwriting on the wall for the V & T.

As it had done for many another short line, the Second World War enabled the V & T to live on what might well have been considered borrowed time. Numbers 25, 26 and 27 rolled the stock cars up and down to Minden in spring and fall, there was an almost daily car of oil for Stewart and the mail and passenger coaches carried more revenue freight than they had in years. Not infrequently, when there were as many as twenty tank or stock cars for morning delivery, the down train was double headed and made a fine show as it poured smoke from twin stacks past the Bowers Mansion and up the grade past Lord Wellesley's estate. There were excursion trains, too, in the old manner of the Miner's Union for the delivery boys of the *Reno Gazette,* the members of the Railway and Locomotive Historical Society, the Lions Club, the California Nevada Railroad Historical Society, and many more. The management even took the road's oldest piece of rolling stock, the little shack car built back in '69, and made it into a club car named "The Julia Bulette" after a celebrated Virginia City strumpet of the seventies. Film companies occasionally hired the road by the day for atmosphere and background shots.

But there was a hitch to the excursion business. The rolling stock was becoming dangerously outmoded and atmosphere seekers wouldn't ride in modern coaches rented from the Southern Pacific. The V & T management was in terror that some serious accident should occur, and the light steel rail, much of it the original article laid in the early years of the road, was worn and in places crystallized. Replacement with modern, heavier iron was out of the question even though ties were replaced when the company's finances permitted and track gangs worked throughout the available months of the year.

Gordon Sampson, general manager after the death of Sam Bigelow, kept his fingers crossed that none of his trestles down Stewart way should burn out, a catastrophe which would probably have ended the V & T then and there. Engine speeds were restricted to five miles an hour on these and they were patrolled after each train during the dry months.

There was one minor windfall. The neighboring Nevada Copper Belt Railroad which precariously connected the now ghost town of Ludwig with Yerington and the Espee at Wabuska, gave up the ghost and Sampson was able to purchase for what amounted to a song its fine engine, No. 5, a sturdy, dependable and comparatively new Alco 2-8-0. To finance No. 5, old No. 25 was sold to the films, and as a minor adventure in bargain hunting Sampson also paid the Copper Belt $250 for an almost new caboose which was painted with V & T colors and added to the dwindling roster of the road's rolling stock. There was even talk of buying a diesel, but the Mills estate in San Francisco wouldn't hear of this prodigality.

No. 5 could haul anything the dispatcher could tie onto it and was equipped with an air horn from the Southern Pacific shops at Sparks. After a while, however, the air horn was abated, at least on the southern end of the run, because its unaccustomed tones set all the dogs to howling and there were a great many dogs in Carson City. During the summer of 1948 business was good and consists of eighteen and twenty stock cars were not infrequent.

There are men still alive who remember the time when terrific blizzards overtook the V & T and when "Washoe zephyrs" piled the drifts so high below American Flat that the little engines were lost for days and when four engines pulling three cars into Reno were wholly invisible under mounds of accumulated snow which ran in mountainous ridges from pilot bar to stack-top and from stack to sand dome.

Dan A. Brown, now of Los Gatos, California, has told the authors something of the old days when he was Wells Fargo messenger at Reno.

> "When No. 22 arrived back at Reno in the late afternoon after its 104-mile round trip to Virginia," he recalls, "its boiler lagging and brass were always as clean as when it started out. It was always wiped and polished at Carson on the return trip.
>
> "One unusual set-up in my time was this: the Southern Pacific's train No. 23 left Goldfield early in the day en route to San Francisco. Traveling north it connected with the Mound House branch at Wabuska, then headed toward the main line which it joined at Hazen. The Mound House branch train, after leaving Wabuska, connected at Mound House with the V & T. If 23 was late at Wabuska, the V & T was late out of Mound House so that the progress of the two trains to Reno was a triangular race with the Espee on one leg of the triangle and the V & T on the other two. When this was the set-up, 'Coonie' Poole, the V & T hogger, always made the train fly like a bat out of hell up the Washoe Valley with its whistle wide open for the grade crossings. The score was about 50-50 over a period of years, but it was a fine sight to see No. 22 all brass and black smoke and glory come tearing into town. In case of a dead heat we men of the Wells Fargo crew in Reno had to work two trains

JAMES GAYNER

HEIR TO A TRADITION OF THE HIGH IRON

As long as it lasted, the V & T combined overtones of big business with the simplicities of a country operation. Here, with the cottonwoods of its spacious and by now grass-grown yards visible through the window, is the main office of the general manager in Carson City depot. At his desk is S. C. Bigelow, a faithful proconsul of the Ogden Mills Estate who held the railroad together on borrowed time long after the lights of the Comstock had dimmed forever and the affairs of short line railroads were becoming increasingly precarious. On the wall behind him is a photograph of the founding Darius Ogden Mills; the properties of the office itself were unchanged in their essential details since the regime of its first and most celebrated general manager, Henry Yerington.

ROLLING STOCK IN REPOSE

At the top of the page opposite is the V & T's ancient bullion car shared at various times by Wells Fargo and the U.S. Mails. In the center is the caboose purchased in the forties from the defunct Nevada Copper Belt for $250, and painted the traditional green and yellow of the V & T. Below is an all wooden tank built by the railroad in construction days in 1869 and, until recently, taking its repose in the shade of Carson yard.

W. A. PENNINGTON

LUCIUS BEEBE

C. M. CLEGG

at once, one on each side of the depot. Sometimes, too, the Nevada-California-Oregon train would arrive at the same time on the other side of town and then we were really in a jam. The V & T was a wonderful railroad, I tell you, in the old days."

Up to the very end the V & T maintained its flavor of the long gone 1870's in its operations, properties and pervading atmosphere. Much of the iron between Carson and Reno was the original Sheffield rolled steel laid down when the road was new. Its stub switches with their red and white painted target stands were never changed in its lifetime of eighty years. The canary yellow and deep Gloucester green of its coaches were the same in 1949 as that which had gladdened the Nevada heart on the first rolling stock long ago in the eighties, although this had originally been painted green in its entirety.

The V & T was something that had survived out of the riding years of the coaches with six horses, the years of the great venturings and interminable landfarings which only the very old men of Eagle Valley remember. When it was new the distances of the old West were great distances and the railroad a greater miracle than anything in the American record until that time. There is nothing in the terms of the twentieth century to lay hold upon the heart and fire the imagining comparable to the first coming of the graded rails.

And if anyone should doubt the heroic proportions of the V & T's importance in the history of Nevada he has but to look upon the Great Seal of the commonwealth, where a V & T locomotive crossing the Crown Point trestle above the hoists of the Yellow Jacket Mine is the heraldic emblem of the state.

Ever since the death of Ogden Mills the shadows have been closing around the V & T. The administrators of the Mills Estate, with the implacable rapacity of the janitors for the absentee rich, had at that time decided on the destruction of the property in the interest of taking a capital loss in taxes, and the mutations of time and the Nevada winters furthered this end so that it was with the utmost difficulty that Sampson was able to maintain operations at all. The tracks between Reno and Carson became so worn that he no longer dared run special excursions even on Nevada Day, the state birthday. In 1948 No. 27 was retired by the inspectors of the I.C.C. It was thirty-five years old and had served its owners well. Broken track and consequent derailments became a daily commonplace. The Mills Estate allowed no funds whatever for new rail or motive power and maintained the operating capital of the railroad at an absolute minimum, refusing adequate finances in the hope that eventually the property would run down like an unwound clock. Rumors of its sale at preposterously low figures circulated widely in Nevada and San Francisco and it was equally widely remarked that either

VIRGINIA AND TRUCKEE RAILROAD.

TIME TABLE NO. 1.

To take effect Monday, July 11, 1870, at 6 o'clock A. M.

For the government and information of Employees only, and is not intended for the public. The Company reserves the right to vary the same as circumstances may require.

TRAINS GOING EAST.							Distances from Carson.	NAMES OF STATIONS.	Distances from Virginia.	TRAINS GOING WEST.						
No. 13	No. 11 Pass.	No. 9	No. 7	No. 5	No. 3 Pass.	No. 1				No. 2	No. 4 Pass.	No. 6	No. 8	No. 10	No. 12 Pass.	No. 14
P. M.	P. M.	P. M.	M.	A. M.	A. M.	A. M.				A. M.	A. M.	M.	P. M.	P. M.	P. M.	P. M.
6.00	**4.00**	**2.00**	**12.00**	**10.00**	**8.00**	6.00	To	....Carson.... 3¼	21	**8.00**	**10.00**	**12.00**	**2.00**	**4.00**	**6.00**	8.00
6.17	4.17	2.17	P. M. 12.17	10.17	8.17	6.17	3¼	...Mexican... ¾	17¾	7.45	9.45	11.45	1.45	3.45	5.45	7.45
6.22	4.22	2.22	12.22	10.22	8.22	6.22	4	...Morgan... 1	17	7.38	9.38	11.38	1.38	3.38	5.38	7.38
6.28	4.28	2.28	12.28	10.28	8.28	6.28	5	..Brunswick..	16	7.30	9.30	11.30	1.30	3.30	5.30	7.30
6.33	4.33	2.33	12.33	10.33	8.33	6.33	5½	..Merrimac.. 4½	15½	7.25	9.25	11.25	1.25	3.25	5.25	7.25
7.00	**5.00**	**3.00**	**1.00**	**11.00**	**9.00**	**7.00**	10	Mound House 2¾	11	**7.00**	**9.00**	**11.00**	**1.00**	**3.00**	**5.00**	**7.00**
7.18	5.18	3.18	1.18	11.18	9.18	7.18	12¾	.....Silver..... 3¾	8¼	6.45	8.45	10.45	12.45	2.45	4.45	6.45
7.40	5.40	3.40	1.40	11.40	9.40	7.40	16½	....Scales....	4½	6.25	8.25	10.25	12.25	2.25	4.25	6.25
7.48	5.48	3.48	1.48	11.48	9.48	7.48	17½	....Baltic..... ½	3½	6.12	8.12	10.12	12.12	2.12	4.12	6.12
7.52	5.52	3.52	1.52	11.52	9.52	7.52	18	Crown Point 1	3	6.08	8.08	10.08	12.08 M.	2.08	4.08	6.08
8.00	**6.00**	**4.00**	**2.00**	**12.00**	**10.00**	**8.00**	19	..Gold Hill... 2	2	6.00	**8.00**	**10.00**	**12.00**	**2.00**	**4.00**	**6.00**
8.25	6.15	4.20	2.20	12.20	10.15	8.20	21	...Virginia...	To	5.30	7.45	9.30	A. M. 11.30	1.30	3.45	5.30

READ DOWN ☞   ☞ READ UP

MR. H. HUNTER, Train Dispatcher, is authorized to move Trains by Telegraph or otherwise. ☞ Trains run daily.
Conductor's attention is called to Special Rules governing the movements of Trains by Telegraph.
No Conductor will leave Carson or Gold Hill without ascertaining if there are any orders, and if all Trains due have arrived.
The **FULL FACED FIGURES** denote meeting and passing places.

H. M. YERINGTON, Supt.

In the year 1963 the great Pennsylvania, advertised for years as "The Standard Railroad of The World" and owning carrier of such celebrated name trains as *The Broadway Limited* and *The Golden Triangle* maintains but nine daily scheduled through trains over its mainline trackage between New York and Chicago. When it hung out its shingle and opened for business in 1870, the Virginia & Truckee, destined to be the darling of fortune and the richest short line in history carded fourteen trains on the round trip between Carson City and the Comstock. Through service to Reno was still in the not too distant future. Perhaps the implications of this comparison are not altogether valid, since the V & T operated at the time over a mere twenty-one miles of trackage and the Pennsylvania's Chicago mileage is close to 1,000 but its suggestions are meaningful. The V & T started business with a bang and maintained it stylishly, profitably and with great success almost to the end of its long and useful lifetime.

W. A. PENNINGTON COLLECTION

LUCIUS BEEBE

the Mills Estate was allowing its sale at a fantastic mark-off in order to avoid the obloquy of abandoning a property from which it had taken such great profits in other years, or that the Estate was taking a shellacking in ignorance of the true potential liquidation value of the railroad.

The pulse of the V & T, as it entered its eightieth year, was beating very slowly indeed.

In the eightieth year of its useful existence, the V & T is still a wonderful and uncommonly beautiful railroad, the most beautiful, many people believe, in the terrain it traverses, of any short line anywhere. The ramparts of the High Sierra have changed only with the seasons since the first year of the V & T's going. Its late afternoon departure from the depot platform at Carson with the ringing of the ancient warning bell swung from the eaves is one of the homely dramas of American existence, a tribute to serene and orderly things in a serene and gently ordered world.

From the high grade at Lakeview the traveler can see the whole of Eagle Valley, the cottonwoods in autumn yellow with the setting sun, the rolling hills beyond, soft in twilight as monstrous mounds of chocolate ice cream. Washoe Lake is a thin sliver of turquoise; the mansion of Sandy Bowers hidden in its corona of Lombardy poplars on the other side of the track. The shadows of Washoe Canyon are deep on the northbound run and by the time the little train has cleared Steamboat and entered the fringes of Reno the lights are on in cottage windows and the smoke of a hundred kitchen fires ascends, vertically, into the Truckee twilight. Parents hold their children on fencetops to see the train's nightly passing.

It is a microcosm of a way of life, vanished perhaps, but infinitely more valid than anything that has yet been devised to succeed it.

When, late in 1948, it became widely rumored that the V & T was to be sold and that its new owner would undoubtedly immediately petition for abandonment, the *Herald Tribune* in far-off New York was moved to editorial comment.

BEGINNING AND END OF A LEGEND

Shown on the opposite page are the first and last locomotives to be enrolled on the roster of the V & T's power. At the top is No. 1, the Lyon, built by Booth & Co. in 1869 at a cost of $16,500. Below, the last engine to come to the V & T was second No. 5, purchased from the abandoned Nevada Copper Belt in 1947 for $4,500. One of the few unnamed engines in V & T history, it is shown here in the morning mixed running in the meadows of Minden.

A LOSS TO THE WEST

It is an unredeemed misfortune that Nevada, a state of rich resources and uncommon natural beauty, despite its affluent history and glamorous frontier legend, should be possessed of no visible trace of sentiment. If it were, it would never permit the abandonment, now threatened, of its romantic and colorful Virginia & Truckee Railroad, a short line that is perhaps better known than any other of Nevada's more savory institutions and one which is celebrated, however indifferent Nevada may be to the circumstance, as a link between the present and the frontier past when Nevada had its beginnings. The V & T, which will be eighty years old next year, has enjoyed a fame far beyond the destiny of most little railroads and is known to all students of Western Americana as the railroad which brought down from Virginia City most of the $600 million in silver and gold which the Comstock Lode produced in its prodigious flowering.

The V & T is no longer the paying proposition it once was, and it is on the cards that it will petition for abandonment and its rails be sold for scrap. The state of Nevada, which could purchase and maintain the railroad which brought its material wealth into being for the amount it takes in taxes from its roulette tables and other amusement sources every few minutes, is indifferent, apparently, to the fate of its last passenger-carrying short line.

If the V & T is sold to the junkman Nevada will have lost another of its holds upon the consideration of the amateur of the historic past and of the tourist who is not in search either of a quick divorce or quick crap game. Nevada may come to regret it.

In the end, however, it was demonstrated that the sale of the railroad to a junking firm would be less justified economically than for the owners to close it and dispose of its assets piecemeal. It was decided that the V & T should be liquidated with dignity and in January of 1949, not quite eighty years from that distant morning when Ike James and Superintendent Yerington spiked the first rail, Gordon Sampson petitioned the Interstate Commerce Commission for permission to abandon.

Well might the *Herald Tribune* be interested in the V & T. The great grandfather of its present owner and editor, Whitelaw Reid, had been Darius Ogden Mills who had for many years pocketed a cool $400,000 a year from the railroad in its profitable heyday. Mills did not approve of the Carson and Colorado but he had always a warm place in his heart for the V & T as had his grandson, Ogden Mills.

What promised to be the last winter of the V & T's existence was one of the most fearsome in the history of Nevada. Temperatures on the ranges dropped to forty below zero and sheep and cattle perished by uncounted thousands or were saved by the most heroic efforts of owners and public agencies. So great was the snowfall in the High Sierra and on the Great Plains that for days at a time no through trains passed over the mainline of the Southern Pacific. The high passes of the Rockies were impervious even to the most powerful Mallets and giant rotaries and at one time no transcontinental passenger train passed through Reno for five days. But the V & T missed no single run and, with a wedge plow ahead and Nos. 5 and 26 in tandem, schedules were made daily, bucking the drifts in Washoe Canyon and achieving their terminals even when there was no mail to deliver.

In the spring there were further elemental excitements. Elsewhere in the West stars fell and great winds blew upon the earth and in Nevada there were hail and thunderstorms of unparalleled violence. Throughout May the heavens opened and the floods came to Washoe, as though, to the mind's fancy, the very skies wept for the passing of the little railroad. Carson Water rose among the ruined dams and millsites of Empire as it had seldom risen when their stamps had been instinct with the wealthy production that was to totter dynasties in Europe and cause Bismarch to order the German Reich off the silver standard.

The hearing of the V & T's official petition for abandonment before representatives of the Interstate Commerce Commission and the Nevada Public Service Commission was held during the first week in May in Carson City before C. J. Peterson, examiner for the I.C.C., and Chairman J. G. Allard of the Nevada public service body, occupying three full days of testimony of a highly technical nature.

The testimony revealed that the V & T had paid no dividends since 1924 and no effort was spared by the management to indicate that the railroad was no longer a paying proposition, although during the past eighteen years the gross revenue per ton mile had risen from $2.10 to $5.16, and that in the judgment of the management there was scant possibility of ever again placing the railroad's operations on a paying basis.

Elaborate exception to these generalities was taken by counsel for Mono, Inyo and Ormsby counties and the Minden Chamber of Commerce, and numerous witnesses for the opposition testified that the proposed abandonment would create hardship, inconvenience and financial loss to all the communities affected by the railroad's freight, passenger and mail service.

Most important of the testimony, according to the space and display accorded it in the daily press, was that offered in evidence by Robert A. Allen, a Carson engineer and former Nevada State highway executive who had been retained by the railroad management as a witness for its

CHARLES CLEGG

A SENTIMENTAL JOURNEY TO WASHOE

When the California-Nevada Railroad Historical Society chartered a "Comstock Express" over the Southern Pacific and brought 450 fans of all ages and degrees of railway sophistication for a last excursion over the V & T over Memorial Day weekend in 1949, every piece of V & T equipment saving only locomotive No. 5 was pressed into service for the occasion. Powered by Nos. 26 and 27, the latter of which was given special permission by the I.C.C. to operate for a single day only, the consist of the special between Reno and Carson included four flat cars with rails and benches built for the occasion, the road's sole remaining box car, its tunnel car, long disused, a flanger, combine, mail car and caboose. Memories of similar excursions long ago to the Bowers Mansion at Franktown, to the pools at Steamboat or to the shady pavilions of Treadway Park in Carson were evoked as the bizarre train and its jampacked occupants rolled noisily across Washoe Meadows and up the grade to Lakeview overlooking Washoe Lake and the stately lawns of Lord Wellesley. The trippers lunched in the V & T shops at Carson where once the chivalry of the Comstock had danced at the great Fourth of July Ball of 1873, exposed untold quantities of film, went on to Minden and Virginia "for to see and to be seen." Shown here are the faithful entrained behind No. 26 and homeward bound on the grade approaching Lakeview.

own case for abandonment at a fee running into several thousand dollars.

Mr. Allen deposed that it would cost approximately $3,500,000 to retrack the entire mileage of the V & T with new ballast and brand new ninety-pound steel rails, to renew its motive power and in general put the railroad on what was suggested by the testimony as being first rate operating condition. No mention was made of the circumstance that sections of the road's trackage are now laid with modern, second-hand rail dated 1922 from the rolling mills, although the greater portion of the road's iron dates from the nineteenth century and is in places crystallized. It was freely commented by Nevadans when Mr. Allen's estimate was brought to their attention in the press reports of the hearing that the rail and roadbed embraced by his appraisal would be sufficient for the accommodation of high speed operations of great density on a main line railroad, but that the requirements of the V & T were somewhat more modest since it only operated a mixed train once a day each way six days a week and that thirty miles an hour was its maximum operating speed.

And while talk of millions was being read into the record in the court room at Carson as the basic requirement for new roadbed and motive power, it did not escape mention outside that No. 5, the V & T's last acquired locomotive and an altogether modern and effective machine, had cost the management no more than $4,500.

Nor, at the time, was any mention read into the sworn minutes of the hearing, although it did not pass entirely unremarked elsewhere, that as a witness for its own abandonment the railroad had retained at a substantial fee an expert who was also Consulting Engineer for the Western Highways Institute, an association of highway truck operators whose members, directly or by indirection, would automatically fall heir to the greater part of the V & T's business should its abandonment be accomplished.

What, more than anything else about the abandonment hearing, more even than the cool acceptance of such fantastic extravagances as the figures cited above, depressed spectators was the attitude of passive resignation to the loss of the railroad expressed in the editorial attitude of the Nevada press. That real estate values in Washoe would automatically approach zero as a limit with the going of the railroad and that substantial industry of any sort would never again consider locating at Carson, Minden or Gardnerville seemed no consideration worth the mention.

It was not until, mistaking an excursion organized by West Coast railfans over Memorial Day weekend and listed by its sponsors as a "farewell to the V & T" for an actual last train, newspapers in California began speaking of the road's abandonment as an accomplished fact that editors in Carson and elsewhere became nettled.

GRAHAME HARDY COLLECTION

"THERE ISN'T A TRAIN I WOULDN'T TAKE"

The great Crown Point trestle of the V & T, spanning the abyss at Gold Hill just a few hundred yards south of the depot, carried trains high above the stacks and hoists of the Yellow Jacket and many other celebrated mines. Folk journeyed long distances to see this engineering wonder and to have ridden across it was almost as important an event as making the grand tour east to Chicago! Perhaps the most social and sociable railroad in history, the arrival of the evening train, such as this might be, from Virginia was a momentous occurrence at Carson and on summer evenings the depot there was usually thronged with strollers taking the air after supper. Through travelers to San Francisco descended from the cars and visited friends and next day's newspaper carried a list of the more important voyagers. There are still living in Washoe men who as little boys were allowed to sit up after supper "until the evening train whistled at the edge of town." This was an established curfew for decades. On the page opposite is a V & T poster in the days when travel between San Francisco and the Comstock ranked in importance with that between New York and Chicago and when sleeper service was regularly maintained through Washoe Meadows where now a daily combine runs in each direction over ties which are fast rejoining the elemental earth.

1876. 1876.

EXPRESS!

New Arrangement, May 1st!

THROUGH TRAINS DAILY BETWEEN

VIRGINIA AND SAN FRANCISCO

VIA VALLEJO.

Passengers go Through Direct Each Way, between

VIRGINIA CITY

AND

SAN FRANCISCO,

via.

VALLEJO.

Tickets Sold, and Baggage Checked

To any point on either Line.

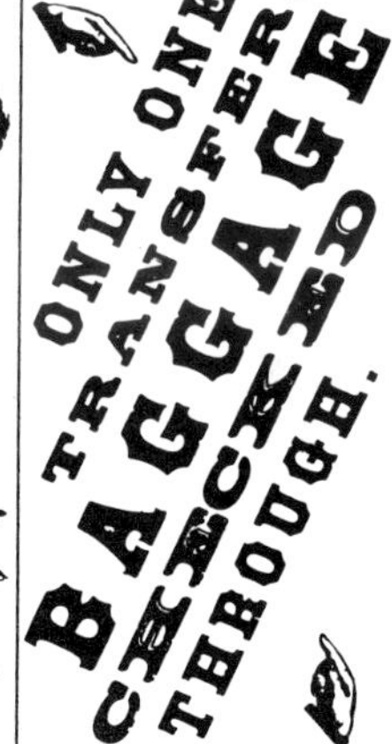

DINNER on Boat from San Francisco, and Breakfast at Carson going East.

H. M. YERINGTON,
Gen'l Sup't V. & T. R. R.

E. NILES,
Gen'l Ticket Agent, V. & T. R. R.

	EXPRESS FROM San Francisco.	JOINT TIME TABLE. VIRGINIA & TRUCKEE AND CENTRAL PACIFIC.		EXPRESS FROM Virginia.
Ar've	9.30 A. M.	Virginia City.	Leave	7.00 P. M.
	9.18 "	Gold Hill.		7.13 "
	8.40 "	Mound House.		7.45 "
Dp. Ar.	8.00 / 7.30 "	Carson.		8.26 / 8.40 "
	6.45 "	Steamboat.		9.31 "
	6.15	Reno.		10.05
	4.10 A. M.	Truckee.		12.00 AM
	9.15 P. M.	Sacramento.		6.30 "
	6.10 "	Vallejo.		9.10 "
Leave	4.00 P. M.	San Francisco.	Ar've	11.10 AM

SLEEPING CAR daily between Carson and Vallejo. BREAKFAST on Boat from Vallejo going West.

A. N. TOWNE,
Gen'l Sup't C. P. R. R.

T. H. GOODMAN,
Gen'l P. & T. Agt., C. P. R. R.

H. S. Crocker & Co.'s Print, 42 and 44 J St., Sacramento.

> Many vitally concerned in the railroad know what proceedings have transpired thus far and that the line's abandonment is far from the sure thing many have been led to believe (announced the even tempered *Nevada Appeal*). None will be too surprised if the V & T is found operating long after the "final excursion" is run. To the claim that the line is expected to "abandon momentarily" the P.S.C. replies that it knows nothing of the "momentary" ceasing of operations. In fact, it was indicated, proceedings of the V & T abandonment may persist for many long months to come.

And the *Virginia City News,* inheritor of the lengendary mantle of the *Territorial Enterprise* of Mark Twain fame, was even less polite in its references to those who, secretly or overtly, hoped for a speedy demise of the railroad.

By the summer of 1949 many of its ancient splendors had vanished from the V & T even as the glory was gone from the Comstock it had served. Departed were the spacious dynasties of the nabobs and bonanza kings who had peopled the overnight Pullmans and Wagner Palace cars from San Francisco. No ear, save that which cherishes the wistful souvenirs of the old days, will ever again detect the songs once sung by the Cornish miners – Cousin Jacks, they were called – who rode the V & T down from Virginia and Gold Hill to picnic at Treadway Park, now also a memory, at Carson. Were he alive, proud old Henry Yerington would never be permitted in a mean generation the $50,000 overdrafts he once drew with such a liberal hand against Wells Fargo & Co.'s banking department.

As the shadows gathered about the V & T and the great days of Nevada railroading merged more deeply into legend a single vestigial trace of heroic times remained in operation across Mount Montgomery Pass in California's remote and beautiful Owens Valley. Here the narrow gage trackage laid with forty pound rails rolled in Holland for Yerington's ambitious little Carson & Colorado continued in operation between Laws and Keeler as a branch of the all-powerful Southern Pacific. Three times a week in ordinary seasons and more frequently in autumn when cattle are being sent to southern ranges, the stock cars and diminutive ore cars bound for the United States Aluminum Company's plant at the little line's northern terminus roll up the valley in shadow of Telescope Peak which once figured so prominently in the annals of the countryside back in the bold bad days of the booms at Panamint, Greenwater and the other commotional bonanzas in the Death Valley region.

The Owens Valley branch of the Espee maintains no passenger service, but for true believers in the narrow gage faith a word in the right quar-

"BLOW, BLOW, THOU WINTER WIND THOU ART NOT SO UNKIND AS MAN'S INGRATITUDE"

Evidence in support of the widely held belief that winters are not what they use to be is implicit in this photograph of the morning down train from Reno as it arrived in Carson City sometime in the thirties behind four engines that have had demonstrably rough sledding in Washoe Meadows and at Lakeview. Other views, believed to have been taken of the same train, at Virginia City show that the same motive power was required to take even fewer cars up the grade to the Comstock since, at this time, two head-end cars were conventionally left at Carson. Below is a smokebox elevation of No. 27 silver painted and mounting a sunflower stack for its last of all runs on the historical society outing over Decoration Day weekend in 1949.

LUCIUS

FRANK (BRONCO) LAZZERI

THE V & T WAS A PICNIC RAILROAD

Sometimes the V & T brought the miners down from Virginia for an evening of dancing and genteel fistfighting at the now vanished pavilions of Treadway Park on the outskirts of Carson, but more often they went to the mansion of Sandy Bowers in Washoe Meadows. Above is an 1890 family group of a Sunday afternoon at the latter classic plaissance, while below Sandy and Eilley Orrum themselves take off from their home on their celebrated trip to call on the Queen and tell her all about Washoe at *her* castle at Windsor, England.

NEVADA STATE HISTORICAL SOCIETY

ters will probably secure permission for a ride in the ancient red painted combine which serves as a crummy and whose trucks were long ago outshopped by the V & T itself in the days when Carson shops could fabricate anything from a cotter pin to a mine hoist. Should the V & T indeed prove a casualty of a greedy generation, the Owens Valley branch will be the last of the once numerous bonanza roads of the old West which came into being with the boom camps and followed the pinched out veins into oblivion.

But even as its sands were running out, the V & T was still, in its venerable age, a silver railroad. Thousands of silver dollars still arrived weekly from the Federal Reserve Bank in San Francisco bound for the vaults of the First National Bank at Carson. Tagged and shipped in canvas sacks of 1,000, they rode down in the baggage compartment of the yellow combine to be met by Chris Nelson's pickup truck at Carson depot and carted off to the bank without even the formality of an armed guard. Until its last train ran the V & T would be a carrier of treasure and wealthy properties.

The passing of the V & T will leave Nevada, in all truth, a graveyard of railroads whose only peer as a necropolis of short lines is Colorado. Forgotten by all but professional railroad historians is the Pioche and Bullionville which was to link that fabulous mining community with Senator John P. Jones' ambitious San Pedro and Salt Lake line. Gone, save in its vestigial remnant, is the Southern Pacific's Owens Valley branch across the state line in California, the once wistful and momentarily opulent Carson and Colorado. With the snows of yesteryear are the Nevada-California-Oregon narrow gage, the Eureka and Palisade of fragrant memory and the once riotous Nevada Central. Only grade rights of way in the southern Nevada deserts serve to remind of the life that once flowed along the Tonopah and Tidewater, the Bullfrog-Goldfield, the Tonopah and Goldfield and the Las Vegas and Tonopah. Dead in the surveyor's reports is the proposed Nevada and Utah Railroad that was to run from Tonopah to the southern littoral of the Great Salt Lake. Closely associated, in California, was the unsinkable Senator Jones' short line, unsurveyed but actually financed, that was to run from San Bernardino over the Cajon to the foot of Surprise Canyon at the height of the fantastic Panamint boom.

When the Virginia & Truckee banks the fires of its engines at last for the long night. as have so many little railroads before it, it will come not again, for the dead return not. But, like the sparkling Concords that went before it down the dusty highroads of yesterday, its memory will live forever in the minds of men, trailing an unforgotten banner of woodsmoke across the Nevada sagebrush where once the railroad ran.

LOCOMOTIVES OF THE VIRGINIA & TRUCKEE

NO.	NAME	TYPE	BUILDER (AND NO.)	YEAR BUILT	CYLINDERS	DIAM. OF DRIVERS	WEIGHT	REMARKS
1	*Lyon*	2-6-0	H.J. Booth (11)	1869	14x22	40 In.	44,000 lbs.	Retired in 1880. Scrapped by V&T after 1900.
2	*Ormsby*	2-6-0	H.J. Booth (12)	1869	14x22	40 In.	44,000 lbs-	See Note 1 below.
3	*Storey*	2-6-0	H.J. Booth (13)	1869	16x24	48 In.	54,000 lbs.	See Note 2 beĭow-
4	*Virginia*	2-6-0	Baldwin (1946)	1869	16x24	48 In.	55,000 lbs.	Scrapped by V&T in 1918.
5	*Carson*	2-6-0	Baldwin (1947)	1869	16x24	48 In.	55,000 lbs.	See Note 2 below.
5	(2nd)	2-8-0	American (66302)	825	19x26	51 In.	150,000 lbs.	Bought in 1947, ex Nevada Coppar Belt 5. Scrapped 1950.
6	*Comstock*	2-6-0	Baldwin (2094)	1870	16x24	48 In.	55,000 lbs.	Sold Aug. 1881 to Oregon Ry. & Nav. 41 for $9,500.
7	*Nevada*	2-6-0	Baldwin (2200)	1870	16x24	48 In.	55,000 lbs.	See Nota 2 below.
8	*Humboldt*	2-6-0	Baldwin (2198)	1870	16x24	48 In.	55,000 lbs.	See Note 2 below.
9	*I.E. James*	2-4-0	Baldwin (2199)	1870	14x22	48 In.	55,000 las.	Sold 1907 to Willett & Burr. Scrapped 1946, Decoto, Cal.
10	*Washoe*	2-6-0	Baldwin (2719)	1871	16x24	48 In.	55,000 lbs.	Sold 1881 to Oregon Ry. & Nav. 42 for $9,500.
#11	*Reno*	4-4-0	Baldwin (2816)	1872	16x24	56 3/4 In.	65,000 lbs.	See Note 3 below.
+12	*Genoa*	4-4-0	Baldwin (3090)	1873	16x24	56 3/4 En.	6?,000 las.	See Note 4 below.
+13	*Empire*	2-6-0	Baldwin (3091)	1873	16x24	48 In.	70,000 lbs-	See Note 5 below.
14	*Esmerelda*	2-6-0	Baldwin (3094	1873	16x24	48 In.	70,000 lbs.	Sold 1901 to Mexican Govt. Rys.
15	*Aurora*	2-6-0	Danforth (884)	1872	17x22	49 In.	71,500 lbs.	Sold 1881 to Oregon Ry. & Nav. 39 for $9,500.
16	*Ophir*	2-6-0	Danforth (885)	1872	17x22	49 In.	71,500 lbs.	Sold 1881 to Oregon Ry. & Nav. 40 for $9,500.
17	*Columbus*	4-4-0	Cen Pac (Sacto 5)	1873	17x24	58 In.	78,000 lbs.	Scrapped by V&T in 1917.
*18	*Dayton*	4-4-0	Cen Pac (Sacto 6)	1873	17x24	58 In.	78,000 lbs.	Snowplow engine. Sold 1938 to Paramount.
19	*Truckee*	2-6-0	Baldwin (3685)	1875	17x24	48 1/4 In.	75,000 lbs.	Sold May 1901 to Verdi Lumber 1 *Roberts*.
≠20	*Tahoe*	2-6-0	Baldwin (3687)	1875	17x24	48 1/4 In.	75,000 lbs.	Sold 1942 to C.C. Bong Const. Co., El Monte, Cal.
+21	*J.W. Bowker*	2-4-0	Baldwin (3689)	1875	14x22	48 1/4 In.	65,000 lbs.	See N/te 6 below.
*22	*Inyo*	4-4-0	Baldwin (3693)	1875	16x24	57 In.	68,000 lbs.	See Note 7 below.
23	*Santiago*	2-6-0	Baldwin (3889)	1876	17x24	48 1/4 In.	75,000 lbs.	Sold Oct 1901 to Boca & Loyalton 3.
24	*Merrimac*	2-6-0	Baldwin (3891)	1876	17x24	48 1/4 In.	75 000 lbs.	See Note 8 below.
25	(1st)	4-4-0	Rhode Is. (2173)	1889	18x26	62 In.	100,000 lbs.	See Note 9 below.
*25	(2nd)	4-6-0	Baldwin (25016)	1905	17x24	60 In.	90,000 lbs.	Sold 1947 to RKO Studios.
26		4-6-0	Baldwin (31341)	1907	18x24	56 In.	121,000 lbs.	Burned in 1950, scrapped.
*27		4-6-0	Baldwin (39453)	1913	18x24	56 In.	121,000 lbs.	Donated to people of State of Nevada in 1950.

H.J. Booth & Co. is also known as Union Iron Works, located in San Francisco.

Surviving Equipment

Presently owned by Old Tucson Studios
+ Presently owned by California State Railroad Museum
* Presently owned by Nevada State Railroad Museum
≠ Presently owned by Railroad Museum of Pennsylvania
ø Presently owned by Virginia City Chamber of Commerce
∞ Presently owned by Orange Empire Railway Museum
± Presently owned by Pacific Locomotive Association
‡ Built into a structure in Carson City

Revised NSRM 5/27/95